ESSENTIALS OF POLITICAL THEORIES & APPROACHES

Essentials of Political Theories & Approaches

By

Durgesh Pande

CYBER TECH PUBLICATIONS
4264/3, Ansari Road, Daryaganj, New Delhi-110002 (India)
Ph.: 011-23244078, 011-43559448 Fax: 011-23280028
E-Mail: cyberpublicationsdelhi@yahoo.com
Website: www.cybertechpublications.com

Essentials of Political Theories & Approaches

Durgesh Pande

First Edition 2011

Asian Offset Printers

Published by

G.S. Rawat for Cyber Tech Publications
4264/3, Ansari Road, Daryaganj, New Delhi-110002 (India)
Ph.: 011-23244078, 011-43559448 Fax: 011-23280028
E-Mail: cyberpublicationsdelhi@yahoo.com
cyberpublications@gmail.com
Website: www.cybertechpublications.com

Contents

Preface

Political science is methodologically diverse, to the discipline include classical political philosophy, positivism, interpretivism, structuralism, post-structuralism, behavioralism, realism, pluralism, and institutionalism. Political science, as one of the social sciences, uses methods and techniques that relate to the kinds of inquiries sought: primary sources such as historical documents and official records, secondary sources such as scholarly journal articles, survey research, statistical analysis, case studies and model building.

As we know any discipline is founded on the pioneering works of many thinkers. This book is devised to present a vivid account of the political thought main approaches in the field. This endeavour consists of the following chapters—Introduction to Political Theory; Elitism; Pluralism; Normative Theory; Marxist Theory: An Evaluation; Democratic Peace Theory; Public Choice Theory; Political Methodology; Miscellaneous Theories; Appendix and Bibliography etc.

Certainly, students, teachers, researchers, political scientists and administrators will find this of utmost use.

With the sole aim of furnishing authentic information, I have consulted piles of literature available in printed or digital forms. I have cited or reproduced vital information from these sources. I am deeply beholden to the authors of these and this publishers as well as copyright holders. Here it is apt to mention the assistance and guidance I received from my seniors, colleagues and family members.

Last but not the least I appreciate the enthusiasm of my publishers to bring out this work within shortest possible time.

I will feel amply rewarded if this endeavour could benefit all those for whom it is meant.

—Author

1

Introduction to Political Theory

> "One should respect public opinion insofar as is necessary to avoid starvation and to keep out of prison, but anything that goes beyond that is voluntary submission to an unnecessary tyranny, and is likely to interfere with happiness in all kinds of ways."
>
> —*Bertrand Russell*

As in this volume we intend to present a vivid account of political theories and political thought, first an account of political science, which will help us understand the themes.

Emergence of Modern Political Science

Since Political Science is essentially a study of human behavior, in all aspects of politics, observations in controlled environments are usually not available and impossible to reproduce or duplicate. Because of this, Political Scientists seek patterns in the reasons and outcomes for political events so that generalizations and theories can be made. Again, study is still difficult since humans make conscious choices unlike other subjects in science, such as organisms, or even inanimate objects as in physics. Despite the complexities, consensus has been reached on various political topics with the help of proper study. To the extent that political scientists are not politicians, they can demonstrate a greater objectivity about politics. Politics may be studied as an activity, as current affairs, as the work of government and as conflict, either national or international, and its early solution.

The advent of political science as a university discipline was marked by the creation of university departments and chairs with the title of political science arising in the late 19th century. In fact, the designation "political scientist" is typically reserved for those with a doctorate in the field. Integrating political studies of the past into a unified discipline is ongoing, and the history of political science has provided a rich field for the growth of both normative and positive political science, with each part of the discipline sharing some historical predecessors. The American Political Science Association was founded in 1903 and the American Political Science Review was founded in 1906 in an effort to distinguish the study of politics from economics and other social phenomena.

In the 1950s and the 1960s, a behavioral revolution stressing the systematic and rigorously scientific study of individual and group behavior swept the discipline. The late 1960s and early 1970s witnessed a take off in the use of deductive, game theoretic formal modeling techniques aimed at generating a more analytical corpus of knowledge in the discipline. This trend has continued and accelerated, even as the behaviouralist revolution has subsided. At the same time, due to the interdependence of all social life, political science also moved towards a closer working relationship with other disciplines, especially sociology, economics, history, anthropology, psychology, public administration, law, and statistics without losing its own identity.

Increasingly, political scientists have used the scientific

method to create an intellectual discipline based on the generation of formal models used to derive testable hypotheses followed by empirical verification. Over the past generations, the discipline placed an increasing emphasis on relevance and the use of new approaches to increase scientific knowledge in the field and provide explanations for empirical outcomes.

It is pertinent to note that political theorists in the past half-century have been primary custodians of a conception of the political as a participatory and rational activity of citizenship. This contrasts with the more usual concept of politics assumed by popular opinion, journalism, and much social science. On this latter view, politics is a competition among elites for votes and influence, and citizens are primarily consumers and spectators.

Hannah Arendt's work remains a milestone in twentieth century political theory because she gave us an inspiring vision of the political as active participation in public life, which many political theorists continue to guard and preserve. In that vision the political is the most noble expression of human life, because the most free and original. Politics as collective public life consists in people moving out from their private needs and sufferings to create a public world where each can appear before the others in his or her specificity.

Together in public they create and recreate through contingent words and deeds the laws and institutions that frame their collective life, regulate their ever-recurring conflicts and disagreements, and spin the narratives of their history. Social life is fraught with vicious power competition, conflict, deprivation, and violence, which always threaten to destroy political space. But political action sometimes revives, and through a remembrance of the ideal of the ancient *polis,* we maintain the vision of human freedom and nubility as participatory public action (Arendt 1958).

Remarkably, Arendt distinguished this concept of the political from the social, a modern structure of collective life which she believed increasingly eclipsed the political. Modem economic forces and mass movements collude to create a realm of need, production and consumption outside the household. Government institutions increasingly define their task as managing, containing and attending to this ever-expanding social realm—through education, public health policy, policing, public administration, and welfare.

People's lives may be well cared for as a consequence, and government more or less efficient in its administration, but according to Arendt in the modern state genuine public life sinks into a swamp of social need (Canovan 1992: chap. 4). Although they often wish to preserve her vision of the political, contemporary theorists have largely rejected Arendt's separation of the political from the social, and her backward-looking pessimism about the emergence of mass social movements of the oppressed and disenfranchised.

The more common judgment is that social justice is a condition of freedom and equality, and thus that the social must be a main focus of the political (Pitkin 1981; Bernstein 1986).

Nancy Fraser recasts Arendt's concept of the social and suggests that much contemporary citizen activism in public life should be conceptualised as politicising the social (Fraser 1989). In this chapter I take up this suggestion, and construct an account of political theory in the last two decades through the theme of the politicisation of the social. The story is of course a construction, from my own point of view, which emphasises some aspects of political theorising in the last twenty-five years, and de-emphasises others. The theme of the politicisation of the social, for example, will lead me to say little about the massive literature in recent political theory which takes some aspect of the historical canon of political theory as its subject.

Much of this scholarship has been influenced by or influenced contemporary concern for social justice and participatory democracy, however. J.G.A. Pocock's *The Machiavellian Moment,* for example, has influenced contemporary civic republicanism. James Miller's reading of Rousseau, to take another example (Miller 1984), is influenced by contemporary discussions of participatory democracy.

The theme of politicising the social aptly organises the great body of recent political theory, providing several illuminating perspectives from which to see these theories. In one way or another, the theoretical trends we discuss either reflect on the conditions of social justice, or express and systematise the politics of recent social movements, or theorise flows of power in institutions outside as well as inside the states, or inquire about the social bases of political unity. Our account divides recent political theory into six sub-topics, each of which expresses a different form of politicising the social: social Justice and welfare rights theory; democratic theory; feminist political theory; postmodernism; new social movements and civil society; and the liberalism-communitarianism debate. Recognising that many works in recent political theory overlap these categories.

Social Justice and Welfare Rights Theory

In 1979 Brian Barry could look back on two decades of

political theory and find the first nearly barren and the second producing bumper crops. With him I will locate the publication of John Rawls's A *Theory of Justice* (1971) as the turning-point. It is no accident that the decade of the 1960s intervened between the barren field of political theory and the appearance of this groundbreaking book.

Despite its rhetoric of timelessness, A *Theory of Justice* must be read as a product of the decade that preceded it. Would civil disobedience occupy a central chapter in a basic theory of justice today? *A Theory of Justice* mapped a theoretical terrain from the thicket of demands and responses to the Black civil rights movement and journalistic attention to poverty: social justice. Rawls insists in *A Theory of Justice,* on the priority of his first principle of equal liberty. Most of the vast literature responding to this book in the last twenty-five years, however, has paid more attention to his second principle, which prescribes equal opportunity in awarding positions and says that social and economic inequalities should benefit the least advantaged. Whether Rawls intended so or not, most interpreted *A Theory of Justice* as recommending an activist and interventionist role for government, not only to promote liberties, but to bring about greater social and economic equality. Hitherto principled political commitment to social equality and distributive economic justice were most associated with socialist politics. Insofar as commitment to such principles had made their way into public policy in liberal democratic societies, many understood this as a result of the relative success of socialist and labour movements in producing certain compromises and concessions from the dominant economic powers (Piven and Cloward 1982; Offe 1984).

A Theory of Justice presented norms of social and

economic equality within a framework that claimed direct lineage with the liberal tradition. A major issue of political conflict in the last two decades, as well as earlier, is about whether a liberal democratic state should legitimately aim to ameliorate social problems and economic deprivation through public policy.

If Rawls supplied the philosophical framework for the side of the debate that advocates public policies directed at improving the relative distributions of the least advantaged, Robert Nozick's *Anarchy, State and Utopia* (1974) supplied a framework for the other. Nozick argues against the use of what he calls "patterned" principles of justice, that is, principles which require public actors to aim at bringing about particular patterns of distribution. Instead he advocates an unpatterned principle, which specifies the procedures through which holdings are legitimately acquired. In Nozick's theory, any pattern of distribution is just which arises from free transfer of initially legitimate holdings.

Nozick finds that conformity with patterned principles requires interfering with consensual economic interaction wherever these would yield outcomes deviating from the desired patterns, and this interference with free exchange makes them wrong. Nozick's is a theory that gives primacy to liberty over any attempts to undermine distributive inequality; Rawls seeks to construct a theory in which commitment to liberty and equality are compatible.

Many articles and collections of essays in the next decade debate the issue of whether a commitment to more egalitarian patterns of distributive justice is compatible with liberty (Arthur and Shaw 1978; Kipnis and Meyers 1985). Several political theorists continue the Rawlsian project of demonstrating that liberty is not only compatible with greater social equality, but requires it.

Amy Gutmann (1980) adds participatory democracy to the values that egalitarian liberalism must promote. Bruce Ackerman (1980) offers a liberal egalitarian conception of social justice that relies on a method of neutral dialogue rather than an imagined social contract. With this dialogue method he re-examines some reasons for questioning a utilitarian theory of justice, and directly refutes entitlement theory's claim that a commitment to collective property and state regulation of distribution is incompatible with liberalism.

Contemporary normative arguments for welfare rights, or a welfare liberal conception of justice, similarly aim to systematise a social democratic political program consistent with liberal values and explicitly refuting more libertarian interpretations of those values.

Remarkably, his idea of social justice as the promotion of people's capabilities, Amartya Sen aims to show the falsity of an opposition between equality and freedom. Equal moral respect for persons implies for development ethics that their capabilities should be nurtured. The most coherent meaning of freedom consists in this nurturing and exercise of capabilities. While Sen's development ethic is egalitarian in the sense of arguing for major redistributive resource allocation to those deprived of opportunities to develop and exercise capabilities, he argues against any simple notion fail equal rights, equal liberties, or the equal distribution of goods, because such notions fail to take account of the variety of human needs and situations.

Kai Nielsen (1985) argues for the compatibility of liberty and equality in a more explicitly Marxist and socialist vein, devoting a large chunk of his Argument to a refutation of Nozick. Even some Marxist-inspired interpretations of justice aim to make an anti-exploitation social and economic theory compatible with a Rawlsian normative theory (Peffer 1990; Reiman 1990). Others insist, however, that different social class positions generate different pictures of society, and different, incompatible, conceptions of justice (e.g.. Miller 1976).

Thus Milton Fisk (1989) argues that liberal egalitarianism is a contradictory normative theory responding to the contradictory social formation of welfare capitalism, and that both are the outcome of an uneasy class compromise. I believe that there is considerable truth in the claim that both the liberal democratic welfare state and a normative theory that attempts to reconcile the liberal tradition with a commitment to radical egalitarianism are fraught with tensions. Perhaps the promised fourth volume of Brian Barry's *Treatise on Social Justice* will further clarify the requirements of just economic distribution.

A long tradition of normative political theory about international relations concentrates largely on issues of war and peace and the adjudication of conflict between states. Perhaps directly inspired by the social divisions that arose around the war in Vietnam, the period we are considering continues that tradition. Michael Walzer's *just and Unjust Wars* (1977) is notable both for its reference to the tradition of just war theory, and its original and creative analyses of distant and recent historical events, including the Vietnam War. More original to contemporary political theory, however, is application of questions of social justice, welfare and distribution to international relations. Charles Beitz argued that Rawls's principles of justice can be used as the basis for evaluating and criticising the distributive inequality between developed societies of the North and less developed societies of the South.

More recently Thomas Pogge has developed a careful and persuasive extension of a Rawlsian approach to problems of global justice (Pogge 1989, pt. 3). Political theorising about social and economic inequality across national boundaries remains underdeveloped. Some important work has begun, however, on immigration issues and international justice (Barry and Goodin 1992; Whalen 1988); environment and international justice (Goodin 1990); hunger and obligation to distant peoples (Shue 1980; O'Neill 1986).

Democratic Theory

Nurtured by social movement calls for participatory democracy in the 1960s and 1970s, in the last two decades normative theorising has flowered that takes speech and citizen participation as central. Carole Pateman's still widely cited *Participation and Democratic Theory* (1970), set much of the agenda for contemporary participatory democratic theory. That work criticised a plebescite and intergroup pluralist conception of democracy, and rearticulated an ideal of democracy as involving active discussion and decision-making by citizens.

It argued that social equality is a condition of democratic participation, and that democratic participation helps develop and preserve social equality. This means that the sites of democratic participation must include social institutions beyond the state in which people's actions are directly involved, particularly the workplace. C.B. Macpherson articulated a framework for critique of the passivity and utilitarianism of dominant conceptions of liberal democracy, and for an alternative more active conception of democracy. It is a measure of how much intellectual discourse has changed in the last twenty years that today reflection on conceptions of human nature seems quaint. Yet Macpherson'* analysis of political theories according to whether they assume the nature of human beings as primarily acquisitive consumers of goods or primarily as developers and exercisers of capacities remains a useful way to orient democratic political theory.

The perspective of possessive individualism will inevitably regard the political process as a competition for scarce goods, where the competitors' desire for accumulation knows no limits. It one redefines the human good as the development and exercising of capacities, then democratic theory takes a wholly different turn.

Distributive justice comes only a means to the wider good of positive freedom, which is itself a social good because realised in co-operation with others. Freedom is the opportunity to develop and exercise one's capacities, and actively engaged citizen democracy is both a condition and expression of such freedom (Macpherson 1973; 1978; cf. Carens 1993).

Macpherson's interest in capacities is similar to Sen's mentioned earlier, and is similarly motivated by a conviction that the meaning of freedom should be deepened in political theory and practice. Several recent political theorists take as a basic value such an expanded notion of freedom, as an absence of domination and positive capacity for self-realisation and self-determination. Equality ca be best understood as compatible with freedom in this sense, rather than in the narrower, usually property-based sense of freedom as liberty from interference.

Thus one aspect of contemporary democratic theory concerns articulation of the conditions of genuine democratic citizenship. People who are deeply deprived cannot be expected to exercise the virtues of democratic participation, and are seriously vulnerable to threats and coercion in the political process.

Too often wealth or property function as what Michael Walzer (1982) calls "dominant" goods: inequalities in these economic relations will generate inequalities in opportunity, power, influence, and the abilities to set one's own ends. So serious commitment to democracy presupposes social measures that limit the degree of class inequality and guarantee that all citizens have their needs met (Bay 1981; Green 1985; Cunningham 1987; Cohen and Rogers 1983).

Most of those who theorise this relation of social and political equality to democracy concentrate on issues of class. Influenced by feminist analysis, however, a few notice the need to address issues of the gender division of labour to support political equality and participation.

Participatory approaches to democratic theory hold that democracy is a hollow set of institutions if they only allow citizens to vote on representatives to far away political institutions and protect those citizens from government abuse. A fuller democracy in principle means that people can act as citizens in all the major institutions, which require their energy and obedience. This conclusion has opened both contemporary political practice and theory to interest in civic associations outside both state and corporate life as the most promising sites of expanded democratic practice. Following Pateman's lead, however, contemporary democratic theory has also shown a renewed interest in workplace democracy. Through practices of workplace democracy, several writers argue, citizens can both begin to realise the social and economic equality that they find a condition for democratic participation in the wider polity, and at the same time live the value of creative self-governance in one of the most regular and immediate aspects of modern life (Schweickart 1980; Dahl 1985; Gould 1988).

The relative impotence of political theory in setting the agenda of political debate may be revealed by the fact that such thoroughly articulated arguments have little influence on discussion of workplace practices. At the beginning of the period the theory of political democracy was largely identified with a theory of interest group pluralism.

Inspired by contemporary participatory democratic experiments and institutions, important critiques of this interest group pluralism emerged with well developed alternative conceptions of democracy based on active discussion. In *Beyond Adversary Democracy,* Jane Mansbridge (1980) argued that conceptualising the democratic process as the competition among interests is too narrow, and she offered a model of "unitary" democracy as one in which participants aim at arriving at a common good through discussion. Wisely, she also argued that unitary democracy has limits, and suggested that both adversary and unitary democracy are necessary in a robustly democratic polity. Benjamin Barber took up the impulse of this classification and critique, but argued in *Strong Democracy* (1984) that an ideal of unitary democracy is too conformist and collectivist. He proposed a model of strong democracy instead, as a participatory model in which citizens form together a public commitment to a common good but where social pluralities of interest and commitment remain. It is not clear, however, that Barber's and Mansbridge's models are all that different. Following these important texts, recent years have seen an explosion of theorising about democracy as a discussion-based form of practical reason. Ideals and practices of democratic decision-making that emphasise reasoned discussion have received important further development and refinement (Cohen 1989; Spragens 1990; Sunstein 1988; Michelman 1986; Dryzek 1990; Habermas 1992; Fishkin 1991; Bohman 1996).

Though this a very important trend in contemporary political theory, as currently articulated the notion of deliberative democracy has at least two problems. On the whole the models too much assume the need for a unity of citizens as either a starting-point or goal of deliberation (Young 1996). Theories of deliberative democracy, moreover, have for the most part not grappled with the facts of modern mass democracy that nurtured the theory of interest group pluralism. In particular, theorists of participatory and deliberative democracy either ignore issues of representation or roundly reject representation as compatible with democracy (Hirst 1990). Representation remains sorely under theorised.

In recent years a few themes have theorised representation in the context of strong democratic theory (Burnheim 1985; Beitz 1989; Bobbio 1984; Grady 1993), but much inure work needs to be done. Future work theorising structures of representation in a large-scale strong democracy would do well to build on the recent *magnum opus* of the patriarch of liberal pluralism himself, Robert Dahl (1989).

Feminist Political Theory

One of the most original and far-reaching developments of political theory in the past quarter-century is work in feminist political theory.

Feminist theorists politicise the social by questioning a dichotomy of public and private and thereby proposing that family relations, sexuality, and the gendered relations of street, school and workplace are properly political relation. It is impossible to do justice to the varied accounts of feminist political theorists in this short space. One theme that runs through much of this work is a deconstruction of the dichotomy of public and private presupposed by both traditional and contemporary political thought. The public realm of politics can be so rational, noble, and universal only because the messy content of the body, meeting its needs, providing for production, caretaking, and attending to birth and death, are taken care of elsewhere.

Male heads of households derive their power to make wars, laws and philosophy from the fact that others work for them in private, and it is no surprise that they would model nobility on their own experience. But a modern reflexive political theory should recognise that the glory of the public is dialectically entwined with the exploitation and repression of the private, and the people restricted to that sphere so they can take care of peoples needs.

However the analysis proceeds, feminist political theory concludes that 20th-century politics requires a basic rethinking of this distinction and its meaning for politics.

Much feminist political theory analyses the masculinism of a universal reason that abhors embodiment and honors the desire to kill and risk life (Hartsock 1983; Brown 1988). Beginning with the ancients, courage tops the list of citizen virtues, which promotes the soldier as the paradigm citizen. Machiavelli is celebrated as the father both of modern *realpolitik* and republicanism because he fashions the account of political man so clearly relying on images of risk, danger, winning, and the competition of sport and battle.

Hannah Pitkin's brilliant study of Machiavelli relies on feminist psychoanalysis as well as critiques of the public-private dichotomy to expose the grounds of this masculinist citizen in a psychic opposition between self and other (Pitkin 1984). Many feminist critics focus on the idea of the social contract to uncover different assumptions about human nature, action and evaluation that exhibit masculine experience and develop a one-sided account of the possibilities of political life and political change. Several have focused on the assumptions of individualism, atomistic autonomy and independence that structure the image of the rational citizen in modern political thought.

Carole Pateman (1988) argues that the idea of the individual assumed by social contract theory is actually male, because that concept of individual ' assumes an independence from bodily caretaking that can only obtain if someone else is doing it for one. Other feminist critics argue that the concept of the rational autonomous individual of social contract theory carries an image of the person as self-originating, without birth and dependence. If the original dependence of all human beings on others were to replace this assumption of self-generation, then the entire edifice that constructs social relations as effects of voluntary bargains would collapse.

Some writers have explored alternative starling-points for a conception of society and the political, which begins with premises of connectedness and interdependence rather than autonomy and independence (Held 1987). Feminists have subjected many of the important terms of political discourse to searching analysis, including power (Hartsock

1983), authority (Jones 1993), political obligation (Hirschmann 1992), citizenship (Dietz 1985; Stiehm 1984; Bock and James 1992), privacy (Alien 1988), democracy (Phillips 1991) and justice (Okin 1989).

Notably, questions and conclusions in this conceptual literature are extremely diverse, but the arguments tend to cluster around two projects. First, feminist analysis argues that theories of justice, power, obligation, and so on reflect male gendered experience, and must be revised if they are to include female gendered experience. Often the criticisn takes the form of arguing that the generality that political theorists claim for their concepts and theories cannot in fact be general because the theories do not notice the facts of gender difference and take these into account in formulating their theories.

Thus Susan Okin argues, for example, that Walzer's arguments about justice become inconsistent when the facts of male domination within communities are taken into account. Second, these conceptual analyses often claim that political theory tends to disembody these central political concepts. Thus Nancy Hartsock argues, for example, that dominant theories of power repress the relation childhood experience of vulnerability, and presume a rigid self-other dichotomy that reduces power to competition and control. Thinking power in terms of embodiment would draw the attention of political theorists to power as power-to and not simply power-over (cf. Wartenberg 1990).

Joan Tronto reflects on issues of power in the context of care-giving and its implications for politics and policy (Tronto 1993). Much feminist discussion about the concept of equality, to take another example, has questioned whether equal respect for women should imply identical treatment to men, because women experience pregnancy and childbirth, and suffer other vulnerabilities because of sexist society (Scott 1988; Bacchi 1991). Feminist arguments about individualism, the public-private dichotomy, contract theory, and the implicit bias in Western ideas of reason and universality have influenced some work of male political theorists concerned with contemporary issues. Much political theory continues using these assumptions, apparently feeling obliged neither to revise their approaches in light of feminist critiques nor lo give arguments against them.

Postmodernism

Notably, many postmodern political theorists concern themselves with the movement and flow of power throughout society, and with how social power conditions and is conditioned by political institutions and conflicts. Second, many postmodern thinkers insist that political actors should be understood as not-necessarily-coherent products of social processes, rather than as unanalysed origins of conflict and co-operation. The work of Michel Foucault stands perhaps most directly as a towering contribution to political theory, at the same time as this work challenges many traditional assumptions. Foucault thinks that political theory and discourse continue to assume a paradigm of power derived from pre-modern experience, and that since the eighteenth century a new structuration of power has operated.

The old paradigm conceives power as sovereignty: the repressive force of a rule's decree of what is allowed and forbidden. The new regime of power operates less through command and more through disciplinary norms. In this modem regime the king and his agents do not reach out from a center to control unruly subjects through fear. Instead, ruling institutions percolate up from the ground, in the outlying capillaries of society, which discipline bodies to conform with norms of reason, order and good taste.

Power proliferates and becomes productive in the disciplinary institutions that organise and manage people in a complex division of labour: hospitals and clinics, schools, prisons, welfare organisations, police departments (Foucault 1979; 1980; Burchell *et al.* 1991). Political theory has yet fully to absorb and evaluate their picture of power as the productive and proliferating process of disciplinary institutions. William Connolly (1987) has taken a leading role in showing Foucault's ideas as a challenge to political theory's uncritical reliance on Enlightenment ideas.

He argues that norms are always double-sided and ambiguous, and that we should resist the bureaucratic impulse to discipline ambiguity. A few political theorists have examined the concept of power in light of Foucault's work (Smart 1983; Wartenberg 1990; Spivak 1992; Honneth 1991). More engagement with Foucault's ideas will require rethinking the concepts of state, law, authority, obligation, freedom, and rights, as well. The critical force of Foucault's analysis is apparent. But this theorising cries out for normative ideals of freedom and justice by means of which to evaluate institutions and practices. Several political theorists make important arguments that Foucault's theorising is implicitly contradictory because he refuses to articulate such positive ideals.

Several other French writers associated with postmodernism have been important for political theory, including Lacan, Derrida, Lyotard, Baudrillard, and Kristeva.

Postmodern thinkers have questioned an assumption that unified individual subjects are the units of society and political action. Subjectivity is a product of language and interaction, not its origin, and subjects are as internally plural and contradictory as the social field in which they live. This ontological thesis raises serious questions for political theory about the meaning of moral and political agency. Interpreting Merleau-Ponty along with some of the others Fred Dallmayr (1981) offers a vision of political process where a desire to control dissipates.

Many writers take up the Derridian critique of a metaphysics of presence (Derrida 1974) to argue that a desire for certainty and dear regulatory principles in politics results in repressing and oppressing otherness, both in other people and in oneself (White 1991). In *Identity/ Differene* William Connolly (1991) gives a twist to this thesis by claiming that *sash* unifying politics produces a resentment too quick to blame and not open enough to ambiguity. Bonnie Honig (1993) applies these sorts *of arguments to* the texts of political theorists such as Kant, Rawls and Sandel she argues that their desire for a unifying theoretical center in political theory oppressively expels subjects who deviate from their models of rational citizen and community.

We find the most important consequence of postmodern critiques of identifying thinking to lie in a reinterpretation of democratic pluralism. Democratic politics is a field of shifting identities and groups that find affinities and contest with one another (Yeatman 1994).

Ernesto Laclau and Chantal Mouffe's 1985 book. *Hegemony and Socialist Strategy,* has been influential along these lines. They argue that the Marxist concept of the revolutionary agency of the working class is a metaphysical fiction inappropriate to the contemporary period of proliferating radical social movements denned by multiple identities and interests. Along fines similar to Lyotard's (1984) analysis of the myth of the People as the subject of historical narrative, Claude Lefort argues that modern politics, especially in relatively free and democratic societies, can rest no legitimacy on a unified "will of the people."

On the contrary, modern democracy is precisely the process of contesting claims ungrounded in any unified subject (Lefort 1986). Radical democratic politics should be understood as the coalescing of plural social movements in civil society, to deepen democratic practice both in the state and society (cf. Mouffe 1993). We endorse a political theory that appreciates social heterogeneity and is suspicions of efforts to unify (see Young 1990). Much of this writing, however, seems either to identify normative standards of Justice and freedom as themselves suspicious, or not to refer to issues of freedom and justice at all. The task for a political theory sensitive to the repressive implications of identifying logic and exclusionary normalisation is to develop methods of appealing to justice less subject to these criticisms.

New Social Movements and Civil Society

In the last years movements have proliferated whose style and demands go beyond claims for rights or welfare: environmentalism, peace movements, group based movements of national resistance and cultural feminism, gay and lesbian liberation. Most paradigmatically, the aim of many of these movements is to politicise the social, to bring many habits of everyday social interaction and culture into reflective question and contestation. Some recent political theory conceptualises the political styles and implications of these sorts of movements, often called "new social movements" (Melucci 1989; Boggs 1986; Moores and Sears 1992). These movements are called "new" for at least two reasons. First, on the whole their issues do not primarily concern inclusion in basic citizenship rights nor the enlargement of economic rights.

Their issues are more specifically social—respect and self-determination for cultural difference, responsibility and pluralism in everyday lifestyle, reflection on power in social interaction, participation in decisions in social and economic, as well as political, institutions. Secondly, the form of organisation of these movements does not replicate the mass movement form of political party or union, a unified bureaucracy seeking power through resource mobilisation.

Instead, these new social movements tend to be networks of more local groups, each with their own principles and style, that nevertheless act in concert *en masse* in some protest actions.

Some important political theory reflects systematically on the normative political principles embodied in some of these movements. The environmental movement, for example, provides substance for reflection on basic normative issues of value, social rationality, and democratic participation.

In spite of the importance of anti-racist social movements emphasising self-determination, full inclusion, cultural pluralism, and reparation for past injustice, political theorists have paid surprisingly little attention to issues of race and racism. Debates about affirmative action have been the most common context for reflecting on issues of racism among American political theorists (Goldman 1979; Bowie 1988; Ezorsky 1991). This focus, while important, is rather narrow. Judith Shklar's (1991) account of the meaning of American citizenship in the shadow of the legacy of slavery gives a more profound place to racist ideology and fears for understanding political discourse.

Bernard Boxill (1984) offers a thorough philosophical grounding for many claims of African Americans about social justice including affirmative action, self-respect, and reparations. Bill Lawson and Howard McGary (1992) conceptualise a political theory of freedom by reflecting on slave narratives. Drawing on the critical reactions of Black feminists and feminists of color to dominant feminist discourse, Elizabeth Spelman (1988) critically questions the use of an undifferentiated category of gender in social and political theory. Along similar lines. Nancy Caraway (1991) synthesises much of the writing of feminist women of color as they dialogue with the ethnocentrism of much feminist political and social theory.

Notably, Andrew Sharp's carefully argued book. *Justice and the Maori* (1990) ; as a model of theorising of indigenous people's movement in the context of advanced industrial society. Some political theorists in Australia and Canada have begun to take up the challenge of normative theorising about indigenous people's issues (Carens 1993; Kymlicka 1993; Wilson and Yeatman 1995). Though there is significant work on indigenous people's issues by legal theorists in the United States (e.g., Williams 1990), we observe few signs of a discussion among U.S. philosophers and political theorists about normative questions concerning indigenous peoples.

Some recent theorising about the role of state and bureaucracy in advanced industrial societies helps set a context for understanding the new social movements. Foucault's theory of normalisation produced by bureaucratised human and social services holds that such operations of disciplinary social power also create their own resistances.

Along some-what different lines, Claus Offe (1984) gives an account of the modern welfare state as having depoliticisied processes of social control and public spending. The state has become an arena where officials conduct their real business more or less behind closed doors, and experts administer policies with a technical know-how that does not bring normative ends into view. Social movements politicise some of this activity from a position outside state institutions. In his concept of the "colonisation of the lifeworld," Jurgen Habermas (1987) offers a theoretical context for conceptualising the meaning of new social movements. State and corporate institutions have developed their own technical rationality which has become "uncoupled" from the every-day life context of meaningful cultural interaction, and then these state and corporate imperatives turn around and constrain or distort the everyday lifeworld.

Many new social movements can be interpreted as a reaction to this colonisation, an attempt to open greater space for collective choice about normative and aesthetic ends, and to limit the influence of systemic imperatives of power and profit. If it is true that state activity is largely technicised, then state institutions cannot function as the site of deliberative politics in advanced capitalist society. Rather, politics, in the sense of people meeting together to discuss their collective problems, raise critical claims about action, and act together to alter their circumstances, happens more in critical public spheres. Outside the state and directed at its actions.

Habermas's major of the early 1960s *The Structural Transformation of the Public Sphere English* edition 1989), has received new attention by political theorists interested in participatory politics and critical normative discourse in late 20th-century society (Calhoun 1991). For the purpose of such theorising, a concept of civil society as the locus of free and deliberative politics has been emerging. The concept of civil society was used in the opposition movements of Eastern Europe throughout the 1980s, and this usage has influenced some of these theoretical developments.

The concept has also been influential in opposition movements in South Africa and Latin America. Leading proponents of the theory of civil society include John Keane (1984; 1988), Jean Cohen (1983) and Andrew Arato (Arato and Cohen 1992). Civil society consists in voluntary associative activity—the array of civic associations, non-profit service organisations, and so on that are only loosely connected to state and corporate economy. Activities of civil society do require a strong liberal state that protects the liberties of speech, association, and assembly. But the activities of civil society are more directly participatory than the way citizens relate to state decision-making apparatus. Both Cohen and Arato and Keane thus look to civil society as the arena for deepening and radicalising democracy. The public spheres of civil society can and should be enlarged by pushing back the bureaucratised functions of the state and structuring more areas of social life in terms of voluntary participatory organisations.

These civic organisations can also serve as the stage from which to launch criticism of state policy and action. The theory of civil society adds an important dimension to our understanding of politics as public action and participation. It also seems to occlude some concerns that appear more salient, however, when the focus is on state policy, namely concerns about economic inequality. The concept of civil society is ambiguous, moreover, about the relation of civil society to the economy.

Not all theorising about civil society and political theory distinguishes between economy and civil society as Cohen and Arato do. Some theorists identify the freedom of civil society with freedom of the market (see, e.g., Kukathas and Lovell 1991). Then the theory of civil society emerges as a new form of anti-state liberalism. Since all civil society theorising agrees that modern welfare state bureaucracies tend to be undemocratic and dominative, the question arises of how a commitment to the active promotion of social justice can be made compatible with this view of politics and democracy.

Liberalism and Communitarianism

Michael Sandel launched the current of contemporary political theory known as communitarianism, which can also be interpreted as politicising the social. Communitarians claims to anchor political values like justice, rights, and freedom, in particular social and cultural contexts. Thus it conceptualises the social as prior to and constitutive of the political. Sandel argued that Rawls's theory of justice wrongly presupposes a moral self prior to social relationships guided by principles of justice, a self unencumbered" by particular culture and commitments into which he or she is thrown. Principles of justice generated from such an abstract notion of self can serve only to regulate public relations among strangers in the most formalistic way.

For a robust political theory of social union, Sandel suggested, justice must be supplemented by recognition of particular community bonds and commitments that constitute selves. In *After Virtue,* Alistair MacIntyre (1981) levelled a more historically oriented challenge to liberalism.

The economic and ideological changes of modem society create a modem dilemma of relativisim Religious and moral questions—questions about the good, the just, the virtuous—have become matters of private conscience or contesting political opinion.

Liberalism is a system of formal adjudication among such competing and incommensurate opinions among which there is no means of deciding some are right and others wrong. In this modern world-view moral agents are released onto the landscape as disconnected, commodified and often cynical atoms. The late modern malaise can best be treated by looking for living communities of shared values and virtues that can serve as contemporary analogues of medieval guild communities, and other traditional self-ruling communities bound by common commitment to particular excellences.

In response to these and other communitarian critiques of liberalism's claim to transcend and bracket particular cultural contexts, some writers claimed that communitarianism implies an unacceptable relativism. If culture shapes norms, and there is no means of gaining a reflective distance for evaluating those norms and articulating principles of liberal reason, then we cannot evaluate morally and politically different social contexts.

Communitarians responded that liberals aim at a dangerous and abstract universality. By the mid 1980s the so-called liberalism-communitarian debate was flooding the pages of journals and books in political theory. But the debate was both too abstract and founded on a false dichotomy. Despite the fact the aim of communitarians was to situate moral and political norms in the particular social contexts of full-blooded agents, they rarely discussed particular communities (cf. Wallach 1987).

It was difficult to find, recover, any communitarian who would reject liberal values of equal respect, freedom of action, speech and association, or tolerance (cf. Gutmann 1985). Few self-proclaimed liberals, on the other hand, were ready to deny the power of particular cultural commitment in individual lives, though they might disagree with communitarians about the normative significance of these facts. The liberalism-communitarianism debate did expose how much contemporary liberal political theory abstracts from social group affiliation and commitment to consider individuals only as individuals. It thus posed an important challenge of whether and how liberal theory ought to include recognition of particular contexts of social and cultural group difference.

Will Kymlicka's *Liberalism, Community and Culture* (1989) represents a turning-point in this debate. Unlike many writings in this discussion, Kymlicka is not abstract about community and culture, but rather discusses the particular cultural and political situations of native peoples in relation to the liberal state of Canada. Staunchly adhering to the values of modern political liberalism, Kymlicka argues that these are not only compatible with, but require, the constitution of cultural rights that may sometimes imply special rights for endangered or oppressed cultural minorities.

The key to his argument that such cultural rights follow from liberalism is his construction of individual rights as including an individual right to cultural membership, and thus to the maintenance of the culture of which one is a member. Another Canadian contributor to this more contextualised discussion of cultural rights, Charles Taylor, is less certain that a principle of cultural recognition is compatible with at least some versions of liberalism (Taylor 1992). If we understand liberalism to require a universality to the statement of rights, such that laws and rules should apply equally to all in the same way, then politically recognising and maintaining particular cultures sits uneasily with liberalism.

The recognition and preservation of minority cultures may require special treatment and special rights for which there are good moral arguments, but arguments beyond the liberal individualist tradition (cf. Young 1989; 1990, especially chap. 6). A different set of recent works has also aimed to produce a reconciliation between the stances of liberalism and communitarianism that were posited in the early 1980s. Liberalism has typically been interpreted as neutral among values and equally accepting of ways of life as long as their activities leave one another alone.

Communitarianism, on the other hand, especially in MacIntyre's version, takes the good, as the ends of action, and virtue, as the disposition to bring about these good ends, as the moral commitment that liberalism has abandoned to relativism. Some writers have rejected the characterisation of liberalism as neutral among ends and virtues, and have argued that liberalism itself implies particular cultural values, normative ends, and behavioural virtues (Macedo 1990; Galston 1991). It is fitting to end our story of two decades of political theory by referring to the same writer with whom I began: John Rawls. The arguments of *Political Liberalism* (1993) are, to a significant degree, attempts to respond to the liberalism—communitarianism debate and the social context of multiculturalism in liberal society.

Rawls moves in the opposite direction from Kymlicka and some of the other writers who aim to reconcile the values of apolitical liberalism with public recognition for particular cultural norms and ways of life. Freedom and respect for particular "comprehensive doctrines," as he calls them, instead requires that they all agree on a set of principles guiding the interaction of distinct communities, but transcending them all.

Multiculturalism is possible in a liberal society only if we re-draw a fairly dear border between what is properly public, the business of the constitutional and legal rules governing the whole society, and what is private, in the sense of matters of individual and community conscience and commitment. Although the overlapping consensus that Rawls believes can emerge from the willingness of different cultures and communities of conscience to set fair terms of co-operation retains attention to social and economic inequality as well as liberty, *Political Liberalism to* constitute a retreat from the social. Rawls thinks that conflicts and ambiguities produced by the being together of concrete communities, about issues of sexuality, family, video content, religious dress in public, and countless other issues, are best handled by re-establishing a legal and political discourse that only admits into its realm issues already framed in terms of generalisable norms-The problem of political conflict in the late 20th century appears to be that particularist value claims of social groups have too much entered public discourse, and we would do better to distinguish those claims that can properly be adjudicated through public reason from those simple differences that are social or private. While Rawls continues to say that the difference principle is important, in this later work he emphasises the procedural mechanisms for arriving at and maintaining committed consensus on civil rights and liberties. Proposals to redistribute wealth and income so as to maximise the expectations of the least advantaged are much more controversial today than they were twenty years ago, even as the ranks of the least advantaged have been swelling. Being less advantaged overlaps significantly, moreover, with social positioning in terms of race, gender, ethnicity, and culture.

Thus rat claims about family values or recognition for cultural minorities were much to do with claims of social justice. Even where less tied to issues of economic disadvantage, the "politics of identity," whereby groups make claims for public recognition of the specificity of their cultural values, are not going away. For all these reasons the current temptation of political theory to retreat from the social threatens to make it even more irrelevant to politics than usual. Fortunately, there are signs that many political theorists will continue engaging with these fiercely difficult political issues of the late 20th century.

The fundamental purpose of theory is somehow to explain, comprehend and interpret 'reality'. Indeed, it is possible to go further and argue that without theory of some sort it is impossible to understand 'reality'. As Zuckerman (1991, p. 118) argues, 'without thinking we cannot perceive -much less describe or explain - the world "out there" . . . . Political Science, like any discipline of knowledge, cannot proceed by observations alone'. Without some idea of what is important, we cannot cut into the seamless web of our world. Theory, in crude terms, helps us to see the wood for the trees. Good theories select out certain factors as the most important or relevant if one is interested in providing an explanation of an event. Without such a sifting process no effective observation can lake place. The observer would be buried under a pile of detail and be unable to weigh the influence of different factors in explaining an event. Theories are of value precisely because they structure all observations.

Theory provides a number of valuable functions in the quest to understand the way the social world works. First, it 'foregrounds' certain aspects of the world and provides a guide as to what to investigate. It enables us to see the world and focus on particular aspects of reality. Second, it acts as a useful 'filing system', a framework within which to place observations of reality. Third, theory enables patterns of ideas to develop. Theories are usually stated in a relatively abstract way, which condenses and systematises experience, allowing us to 'make some coherent sense of multiple bits of information' A good theory not only meets some observational tests but also has a logical coherence and a depth. It links together, in a complex whole, a set of ideas and hypotheses. Finally, theory facilitates debate, exchange and learning within political science. Theoretical statements enable the identification of common ground as well as divergence and discrepancies between contrasting patterns of ideas.

The practice of theorising takes a variety of forms within political science. An initial distinction can be made between normative and empirical theories. *Normative Theories* are theories about how the world ought to be; the theorist posits a desired set of conditions and argues why it is preferred. Normative theory is concerned with 'the bearing or promoting of norms, in the sense of values'. Closely related, are two types of theory that try to link values to 'facts'. *Prescriptive Theories* are instrumental: they are concerned with the best means of achieving a desired condition. *Evaluative theory* assesses a given condition by reference to a set of concepts and values.

The *Descriptive-Empirical* approach constitutes the other broad camp in theory-making. It is concerned with building an explanation based on the 'facts'. In a narrow sense, empirical theory is concerned with establishing causal relationships - what factors (independent variables) account for the phenomenon to be explained (dependent variable). In its strictest form the *causal theory* should be framed in such a way as to be capable of empirical falsification. A related variant of empirical theory operates on a deductive rather than an inductive basis. *Predictive* theorising starts with a set of premises and deduces conclusions about behaviour from these premises. While the assumptions underlying the theory may not be valid or verifiable empirically, it is argued that they lead to accurate predictions (explanations) about behaviour.

In a broader sense, empirical theory is about providing an understanding of reality. Theory in this sense can take the form of *models or conceptual frameworks.* Models are representations or stylised, simplified pictures of reality. They identify important components of a system but do not posit relationships among variables. Conceptual frameworks or perspectives provide a broad language and a form of reference in which reality can be examined. They go further than a model in providing interpretations of relationships between variables. Conceptual frameworks achieve a greater depth and breadth in their attempts to explain reality.

Normative theorists obviously concentrate on normative theory and its sub-sets. Institutional studies and feminist analysis are the most catholic in their tastes, offering all varieties with the general exception of predictive theory. A concern with predictive capability is characteristic of rational choice theory. Behaviouralists favour the generation of causal, falsifiable empirical theory. The broader style of empirical theorising is favoured by the other four approaches, excluding that is, normative theory.

The forms taken by theory in political science are diverse and so, not surprisingly, is the content. Another related reason for a focus upon theories of the state is because of the overarching and organising role they have played within political science over the past three decades. As Dunleavy (1987) argues theories of the state have emerged as a central linking element in contemporary political science and have helped to generate a substantial body of theory - guided research in a diverse range of fields within the discipline.

In the next chapter we will discuss different theories in elaborate way.

REFERENCES

Allen, A. 1988. *Uneasy Access: Privacy far Women in a Free Society.* Totowa, N.J.: Rowman and Littlefield.

Arato, A., and Cohen, J. 1992. *Civil Society and Political Theory.* Cambridge, Mass.: MIT Press.

Arendt, H. 1958. *The Human Condition.* Chicago: University of Chicago Press.

Arthur, J., and Shaw, W., eds. 1978. *Justice and Economic Distribution.* Englewood Cliffs, N.J.: Prentice-Hall.

Bacchi, C. 1991. *Same Difference.* Boston: Alien and Unwin.

Barber, B. 1984. *Strong Democracy.* Berkeley; University of California Press.

Barry, B. 1979. The strange death of political philosophy. Pp. 11-23 in *Democracy, Power and Justice.* Oxford: Clarendon Press, 1989.

—— 1989. *A Treatise on Social Justice.* Vol. I. *Theories of Social Justice.* Berkeley: University of California Press.

Bay, C. 1981. *Strategies of Political Emancipation.* Notre Dame, Ind.: University of Notre Dame Press.

Beitz, C. 1979. *Political Theory and International Relations.* Princeton: Princeton University Press.

Bernstein, R. 1986. Rethinking the social and the political. Pp. 238-59 in R. Bernstein, *Philosophical Profiles.* Philadelphia, Pp.: University of Pennsylvania Press.

Bobbio, N. 1984. *The Future of Democracy.* Minneapolis: University of Minnesota Press.

Bock, G., and James, S., eds. 1992. *Beyond Equality and Difference.* London: Routledge.

Boggs, C. 1986. *Social Movements and Political Power.* Philadelphia, Pa.: Temple University Press.

Bohman, J. 1996. *Public Deliberation.* Cambridge, Mass.: MIT Press.

Bowis, N., 1988, *Equal Opportunity.* Boulder, Colo.: Westview Press.

Boxill, B. 1984 *Blacks and Social Justice.* Totowa, N.J.: Rowman and Allenheld.

Brown, W. 1988. *Manhood and Politics.* Totowa, N.J.: Rowman and Littlefield.

Burchell, G.; Gordon, C.; and Miller, P., eds. 1991. *The Foucault Effect.* Chicago: University of Chicago Press.

Burnheim, J. 1985, *Is Democracy Possible?* Oxford: Polity Press.

Calhoun, C. ed 1991. *Habermas and the Public Sphere.* Cambridge, Mass.: MIT Press.

Canovan, M. 1992. *Hannah Arendt: A Reinterpretation of Her Political Thought.* Cambridge: Cambridge University Press.

Caraway, N. 1991. *Segregated Sisterhood.* Nashville: University of Tennesee Press.

Carens, J.H. 1993. Citizenship and aboriginal self-government. Ottawa, Ont.: Royal Commission on Aboriginal Peoples.

—— ed. 1993. *Democracy and Possessie Individualism.* Albany: State University of New York Press.

Clark, L., and Lange, L. 1979. *The Sexism of Social and Political Theory.* Toronto: University of Toronto Press.

Cohen, J. 1983. Class and Civil Society. Amherst: University of Massachusetts Press.

—— 1989. Deliberation and democratic legitimacy. Pp. 17-34 in *The Good Polity,* ed. A. Hamlin and P. Pettit. Oxford: Blackwell.

—— and Rogers, J. 19083. *On Democracy.* New York: Penguin.

Connolly, W.E. 1987. *Politics and Ambiguity*. Madison: University of Wisconsin Press.

—— 1991. *Identity Difference*. Ithaca, N.Y.: Cornell University Press.

Cunningham, F. 1987. *Democratic Theory and Socialism*. Cambridge: Cambridge University Press.

Dani, R.A. 1985. *A Preface to Economic Democracy*. Berkeley: University of California Press.

—— 1989 *Democracy and Its Critics*. New Haven, Conn.: Yale University Press.

Dallmayr, F. 1981. *Twilight of Subjectivity*. Amherst: University of Massachusetts Press.

Derrida, J. 1974. *Of Grammatology*, trans. G.C. Spivak. Baltimore, Md.: Johns Hopkins University Press.

Dietz, M. 1985. Citizenship with a feminist face: the problem with maternal thinking. *Political Theory*, 13: 19-37.

Dayzek, J. 1987. *Rational Ecology*. Oxford: Basil Blackwell.

—— 1990. *Discursive Democracy*. Cambridge: Cambridge University Press.

Elshtain, J.B. 1981. *Public Man, Private Woman*. Princeton, N.J.: Princeton University Press.

Ezorsky, G. 1991. *Racism and Justice*, Ithaca, N.Y.: Cornell University Press.

Fishkin, J.S. 1991. *Deliberative Democracy*. New Haven, Conn.: Yale University Press, 1991.

Fisk, M. 1989. *The State and Justice*. Cambridge: Cambridge University Press.

Foucault, M. 1979. *Discipline and Punish*, trans. A Sheridan. New York: Vintage Books.

—— 1980. *Power/Knowledge*, trans. and ed. C. Gordon, L. Marshall, J. Mephan and K. Soper. New York: Pantheon Books.

Fraser, N. 1989. *Unruly Practices*. Minneapolis: University of Minnesota Press.

Galston, W. 1991. *Liberal Purposes*. Cambridge: Cambridge University Press.

Goldman, A. 1979. *Justice and Reverse Discrimination*. Princeton, N.J.: Princeton University Press.

Goodin, R.E. 1988. *Reasons for Welfare.* Princeton, N.J.: Princeton University Press.

—— 1990. International ethics and the environmental crisis. *Ethics and International Affairs,* 4: 91-105.

Goodin, R.E. 1992. *Green Political Theory.* Oxford: Polity Press.

Gould, C. 1988. *Rethinking Democracy.* Cambridge: Cambridge University Press.

Grady. R. C. 1993. Restoring *Real Representation.* Urbana: University of Illinois Press.

Green, P. 1985. *Retrieving Democracy.* Totowa, N.J.: Rowman and Allenheld.

Gutmamn. A. 1980. *Liberal Equality.* Cambridge: Cambridge University Press.

—— 1985. Communitarian critics of liberalism. *Philosophy and Public Affairs,* 14:308-22. habermas. I. 1987. *The Theory of Communicative Action,* trans. T. McCarthy. Boston: Beacon Press.

——1989. *The Structural Transformation of the Public Sphere,* trans. T. Burger with F. Lawrence. Cambridge: MIT Press; originally published 1962.

—— 1990. *The Philosophical Discourse of Modernity.* Cambridge, Mass.: MIT Press.

——1992. *Faktizitat und Geltung.* Frankfurt Suhrkamp Verlag. English translation: *Between Facts and Norms,* trans. W. Rehg. Cambridge, Mass.: MIT Press, forthcoming.

Hartsock, N. 1983. *Money. Sex and Power.* New York: Longman.

Held, V. 1987. Non-contractual society. Pp. 111-38 in *Science, Morality and Feminist Theory,* ed. M. Hanen and K. Nielsen. Calgary: University of Calgary Press.

Hirschmann, N. 1992. *Rethinking Obligation.* Ithaca, N.Y.: Cornell University Press.

Hirst, P. 1990. *Representative Democracy and its Limits.* Oxford: Polity Press.

Honig, B. 1993. *Political Theory and the Displacement of Politics.* Ithaca, N.Y.: Cornell University Press.

Honneth, A. 1991. *The Critique of Power.* Cambridge, Mass.: MIT Press.

Jones, K. 1993. *Compassionate Authority.* New York Routledge.

Keane, J. 1984. *Public Life in Late Capitalism.* Cambridge: Cambridge University Press.

——1988. *Democracy and Civil Society.* London: Verso.

Kipnis, K., and Meyers, D. T., eds. 1985. *Economic Justice: Private Rights and Public Responsibilities.* Totowa, N.J.: Rowman and Allenheld.

Kukathas, C., and Lovell, D. W. 1991. The significance of civil society. Pp. 18-40 in *The Transition from Socialism,* ed. C. Kukathas, D. W. Lovell and W. Maley, Sydney: Longman Cheshire.

Kymlicka, W. 1989. *Liberalism, Community and Culture.* Oxford: Clarendon Press.

Laclau, E., and Mouffe, C. 1985. *Hegemony and Socialist Strategy.* London: Verso.

Landes, J. 1988. *Women and the Public Sphere in the Age of the French Revolution.* Ithaca, N.Y.: Cornell University Press.

Lawson, B., and McGary, H. 1992. *Between Slavery and Freedom.* Bloomington: Indiana University Press.

Lefort, C. 1986. *The Political Forms of Modem Society.* Cambridge: Cambridge University Press.

Lyotard, I.-F. 1984. *The Postmodern Condition.* Minneapolis: University of Minnesota Press.

Macedo, S. 1990. *Liberal Virtues.* Cambridge, Mass.: Harvard University Press.

MacIntyre, A. 1981. *After Virtue.* Notre Dame, Ind.: Notre Dame University Press.

Macpherson, C. B. 1973. *Democratic Theory.* Oxford: Clarendon Press.

Mansbridge, I. J. 1980. *Beyond Adversary Democracy.* New York Basic Books.

Melucci, A. 1989. *Nomads of the Present* London: Hutchinson Radius.

Michelman, F. 1986. Traces of self-government. *Harvard Law Review,* 100:1-311.

References

Miller, D. 1976. *Social Justice.* Oxford: Clarendon Press.

Miller, J. 1984. *Rousseau: Dreamer of Democracy*. New Haven, Conn.: Yale University Press.

Moers, C., and Sears, A. 1992. The new social movements and the withering away of state theory. Pp. 52-68 in *Organising Dissent,* ed. W.K. Carroll. Toronto: Garamond Press.

Mouffe, C. 1993. *The Return of the Political.* London: Verso.

Nicholson, L. 1986. *Gender and History*. New York: Columbia University Press.

Nielsen, K. 1985. *Equality and Liberty*. Totowa, N.J.: Rowaman and Allanheld.

Nozick, R. 1974. *Anarchy, State and Utopia.* New York: Basic Books.

O'Neili, O. 1986. *Faces of Hunger*. London: Allen and Unwin.

Offe, C. 1984. *Contradictions of the Welfare State.* Cambridge, Mass.: MIT Press.

Okin, S.M. 1988. *The Sexual Contract.* Standord, Calif.: Stanford University Press.

Peffer, R. 1990. *Marxism, Morality, and Social Justice.* Princeton, N.J.: Princeton University Press.

Phillips, A. 1991. *Engendering Democracy.* University Park, Penn : Penn State Press.

Pitkin, H.F. 1984. *Fortune is a Woman.* Berkeley: University of California Press.

Prven, F.F., and Cloward, R. 1982. *The New Class War.* New York: Pantheon.

Pocock, J.G.A. 1975. *The Machiavellian Moment.* Princeton, N.J.: Princeton University Press.

Pogge, T.W. 1989. *Realising Rawl.* Ithaca, N.Y.: Cornell University Press.

Rawls, J. 1971. *A Theory of Justice.* Cambridge, Mass.: Harvard University Press.

—— 1993. *Political Liberalism.* New York: Columbia University Press.

Reiman, J. 1990. *Justice and Modern Moral Theory.* New Haven, Conn.: Yale University Press.

Sagoff, M. 1988. *The Economy of the Earth.* Cambridge: Cambridge University Press.

Sandel, M.J. 1982. *Liberalism and the Limits of Justice.* Cambridge: Cambridge University Press.

Schweickart, D. 1980. *Capitalism or Worker Control?* New York: Paeger.

Scorrr, J.W. 1988. Deconstructing equality versu difference: or, the uses of poststructuralist theory for feminism. *Feminist Studies,* 14: 33-50.

Sen, A.K. 1992. *Inequality Reconsidered.* Oxford: Oxford University Press.

Shanley, M.L., and Pateman, C., eds. 1991. *Feminist Interpretations and Political Theory.* University Park, Pa.: Penn State Press.

Sharp, A. 1990. *Justice and the Maori.* Auckland: Oxford University Press.

Shklar, J. 1991. *American Citizenship.* Cambridge, Mass.: Harvard University Press.

Shue, H. 1980. *Basic Rights.* Princeton, N.J.: Princeton University Press.

Smart, B. 1983. *Foucault, Marxism and Critique.* London: Routledge and Kegan Paul.

Smith, R. 1989. "One united people:" second-class female citizenship and the American quest for community. *Yale Journal of Law and Humanities,* 1/2:229-93.

Spelman, E. 1988. *Inessential Woman.* Boston: Beacon Press.

Spivak, G.C. 1992. More on power/knowledge. Pp. 149-73 in *Rethinking Power,* ed. T.E. Wartenberg. Albany: State University of New York Press.

Spragens, T. 1990. *Reason and Democracy.* Durham, N.C.: Duke University Press.

Sterba, J. 1988. How to *Make People Just.* Totowa, N.J.: Rowman and Littlefield

Stiehm, J., ed. 1984. *Women's Views of the Political World of Men.* Dobbs Ferry, N.Y.: Transnational Publishers.

Sunstein, C. 1988. Beyond the republican revival. *Yale Law Journal,* 97:1539-90.

Taylor, C. 1984. Foucault on freedom and truth. *Political Theory,* 12:152-83.

Tronto, J. 1993. *Moral Boundaries.* New York Routledge.

Wallach, J. 1987. Liberalism, communitarians and the tasks of political theory. *Political Theory,* 15: 581-611.

Walzer, M. 1977. *Just and Unjust Wars.* New York: Basic Books.

Wartenberg, T. 1990. *Forms of Power.* Philadelphia, Pa.: Temple University Press.

Wellmam, C. 1982. *Welfare Rights.* Totowa, N.J.: Rowman-and Allenheld.

White, S. 1991. *Political Theory and Postmodernism.* Cambridge: Cambridge University Press.

Williams, R. A. 1990. *The American Indian in Western Legal Thought.* Oxford: Oxford

University Press. wilson, M., and yeatman, A., eds. 1995. *Justice and Identity.* Wellington, N.Z.: Bridget Williams.

Yeatman, A. 1994. *Postmodern Revisionings of the Political.* New York: Routledge.

Young, I.M. 1987. Impartiality and the civic public some implications of feminist critiques of moral and political theory. Pp. 56-76 in (ed.) S. Benhabib and D. Cornell. Minneapolis: University of Minnesota Press.

2

Elitism

> "A Dwarf standing on the shoulders of a Giant sees further than the Giant; but if he stood upon his own basis, he would scarcely see at all. It behooves him to remember that the Giant is a Giant."
>
> — ***Lewis***

In the present chapter we will elucidate 'elite doctrine' of political theory.

First is remarkable that at the core of the elitist doctrine lies the belief that the history of politics is the history of elite domination. Elitist theory therefore challenges the key premises of most Western liberal assumptions about politics, the organisation of government and the 'proper' relationship between the state and civil society. As Gaetano Mosca (1939, p. 50) puts it:

> "In all societies — from societies that are very meagrely developed and have barely attained the dawnings of civilisation, down to the most advanced and powerful societies - two classes of people appear - a class that rules and a class that is ruled. The first class, always the less numerous, performs all political functions, monopolises power and enjoys the advantages that power brings, whereas the second, the more numerous class, is directed and controlled by the first."

Hence, the nature of any society — whether it is consensual or authoritarian, dynamic or static, pacifist or totalitarian, legitimate or illegitimate — is determined by the nature of its elite. Moreover, the goals of every society are both established and manipulated by its elite (Prewitt and Stone, 1973, p. 3).

Here our aim is to review the content and nature of elite theory. The scope of the chapter is circumscribed by space: it is by no means exhaustive, nor does it attempt to be. Broadly this argues that the elitist position is a cumulative one which rests on three central claims: a belief in the inevitability of elite rule and the irrationality of liberal democracy; a rejection of the economistic Marxist conception of the economy as the ultimate determinant of societal dynamics; and a belief in the potential autonomy of the state from social and economic forces.

1. Classical Elitism

No doubt, the seeds of the perspective were sown in the ideas of Plato, Niccolo Machiavelli and others, elitism as a theory of social power is most associated with the works of Vilfredo Pareto, Gaetano Mosca and Robert Michels. Their common thesis was that the concentration of social power in' a, small set of controlling elites was inevitable in all societies, and they rejected the feasibility of Karl Marx's vision of evolutionary change towards a classless society with power equality.

Pareto argued that historical experience provides testimony to the perpetual circulation of elites and oligarchy. Every field of human enterprise has its own elite, Pareto borrowed two categories of elites from Machiavelli: 'foxes' and 'lions' (Pareto, 1966, pp. 99, 110), in order to illustrate the nature of governing elite structures. The two categories stand at opposite ends of a continuum of governance. 'Foxes' govern by attempting to gain consent and are not prepared to use force, they are intelligent and cunning, enterprising, artistic and innovative. However, in rimes of crisis their misplaced humanitarianism leads them towards compromise and pacifism.

Hence, when final attempts to reach a political solution have failed, the regime is fatally weakened. 'Lions' represent the opposite pole. They are men of strength, stability and integrity; cold and unimaginative, they are self-serving and are prepared to use force to achieve or maintain their position. 'Lions' are defenders of the status quo in both the state and civil society. They are likely to be committed to public order, religion and political orthodoxy. For Pareto, the qualities of 'fox' and 'lion' are generally mutually exclusive.

History is a process of circulation between these two types of elite. Pareto's ideal system of governance would reflect a balance of forces that exhibits characteristics of both 'fox' and 'lion'. This incessant process of elite renewal, circulation and replacement illuminates the thesis that an elite rules in all organised societies. Pareto's focus on the concentration of power in the hands of a political elite represented a rejection of both vulgar Marxist economism and the weak but popular liberal/pluralist view. It undermined the Marxist conception of the state as a mere tool of the working class. It rejects Marx's claim (Marx, 1983, p. 203) that 'the history of all hitherto existing society is the history of class struggle'. Within this approach, liberal-democratic constitutions give expression to bourgeois demands and cement the dominant ideology.

Hence, for Marxists, the state is a reflection of the

economic conditions and the nature of class struggle. No capitalist state can be called democratic in the sense of securing liberty and rendering the exercise of political power accountable because the state ensures the long-term interests of continued and expanding capital accumulation. At the same time, Pareto's elitist claims also weaken the pluralist conception of the state as a co-ordinator of the national interest in a plural society.

Within the pluralist paradigm the polity is comprised of a multiplicity of competing groups, all of which seek to influence the decision-making process. Rule purports to be in the interest of all and not that of any one section or alliance of sections. The duty of government is to harmonise and co-ordinate. Mosca argued that elites were inevitable as all societies are characterised by the dictatorship of the majority by the minority. He posited the existence of a ruling, but not necessarily economically dominant, class from which key office holders were drawn.

Within Mosca's formulation, each ruling class develops a 'political formula' which maintains and legitimates its rule to the rest of the population. Elite circulation will usually occur through inheritance but, from time to time, power will pass into the hands of another class due to the failure and collapse of the 'political formula'. Mosca's conceptualisation of the 'political formula' has much in common with the concept of 'hegemony', which springs from the views of Karl Marx and Friedich Engels in *The German Ideology* (1846); the ideas of the ruling class are in every historical stage the ruling ideas. Hence, the class that is the dominant economic group in society is, at the same time, its ruling intellectual force (Evans, 1975, pp. 82-6).

In other words, an economistic Marxist would say that those people owning the means of production also control the process of government and can use this domination to impose their views on society. This results in a false consciousness among the proletariat, whereby they accept their subordinate position in capitalist society and do not question the existing social and political structure. Mosca failed to develop the concept of 'political formula' in any systematic way, unlike his Marxist contemporary, Antonio Gramsci.

The centrality of the ideological dimension to an understanding of the dialectic of power domination and control is an important consideration that Mosca's research clearly overlooked. Michels' work needs to be understood in the context of his own personal struggle against the German academic establishment. He wrote from the standpoint of a radical socialist whose ability to secure an academic post— a German university was impared by his ideological position. However, it was the German Social Democratic Party, and its propensity for oligarchy, and not the establishment, that bore the full brunt of his frustrations.

Michels' (1962, p. 364) central explanation of the inevitability of elites represents a further critique of pluralism and Marxism. With regard to the former, Michels argued that the practical ideal of democracy consisted in the self-government of the masses in conformity with the decision-making of popular assemblies. However, while this system placed limits on the extension of the principle of delegation, it fails, 'to provide any guarantee against the formation of an oligarchial camerilla' [political structure].

In short, direct government by the masses was impossible. Michels applied a similar argument to political parties. In his view, the technical and administrative functions of political parties make first bureaucracy and then oligarchy inevitable. Hence, for Michels (1962, p. 364), 'Who says organisation, says oligarchy.' This maxim clearly determined his conception of the nature of elites. The notorious notion of the 'iron law of oligarchy' provides the key to Michels' thoughts on the nature of elite structures, because it ensures the dominance of the leadership over the rank and file membership.

Elite circulation is maintained by the inability of the masses to mobilise against the leadership view. This ensures their subjugation to the whim of the elite. In essence, it is the very existence of this system of leadership that is incompatible with the tenets of liberal democracy and pluralism.

Notably, work of Robert Michels is remembered more as a series of sound bites than as a seminal contribution to political thought. As a case in point, his phrase the 'iron law of oligarchy' has been conceptualised more by others than by himself-' For example, the notion of organisation as the basis of oligarchy has been developed much further in the research of Max Weber (1947) and organisational theorists such as March and Simon (1958), among others. The major impact of Michels' work has been on pluralist thinking in so far as it has compelled pluralists to acknowledge the existence of elites, although they continue to reject the argument that elites act cohesively. The integration of elites is generally assumed by Pareto, Mosca and Michels without any rigorous empirical investigation. Pareto failed to demonstrate a theory of elite domination in his native Italy. Mosca showed that governments in the past were often characterised by a self-serving elite, but did not establish that this was always the case. Further, while Michels argued that Western European political parties were characterised by elite domination, it was a difficult proposition to sustain empirically. Perhaps not surprisingly, then, subsequent elite theorists have disagreed strongly about the relative degree, causes and consequences of elite integration in Western industrialised societies.

In the USA a lengthy debate hat ensued over the structure of power and influence at the national level, which has centred on the degree to which this structure of elite domination ..as coalesced or expanded (see Moore, 1979). This debate will be considered in the third section of this chapter.

2. Democratic Elitism

In fact, Democratic elitism is associated with the work of Max Weber (1864-1920) and Joseph Schumpeter (1883-1946) which emerged in critique of the weak liberal view of democratic theory. Both these thinkers believed that participation in politics was circumscribed by powerful social forces. In their view, liberal democracy at its very best was a restrictive enterprise for selecting decision-makers and ensuring their legitimacy through elections.

At worst, it was an attenuated form of governance aimed at securing the hegemony of a ruling political elite. Max Weber's political thought emphasises the independent influence of the 'political' as opposed to the 'economic'. He therefore rejected any notion that the history of ideas could be reduced to economic factors. Hence he was opposed to Marxist analyses of 'ideology' and 'superstructure'.

He further argued that the advance of bureaucratic organisation was an inevitable component of the growth of capitalism and had undermined the efficacy of the liberal democratic model. He viewed democracy as a means for securing good government rather than popular control and political equality and refuted any natural law of democratic government embodied in classical democratic theory. Weber's views on state power and domination are central to our understanding of the theoretical development of elitist thought. They represent a significant and sophisticated development.

> Weber argued that the state is characterised by three main elements:
>
> - a differentiated set of institutions and personnel;
> - centralisation, in the sense that political relations radiate from the centre to cover a territorially demarcated area; and
> - a monopoly of authoritative, binding rule-making sustained by a monopoly of the means of physical violence (Mann, 1988, p. 4).

Remarkably, for Weber, elite domination within the state apparatus was inevitable. As Weber himself puts it, 'All ideas aiming at abolishing the dominance of men over men are illusory' (Weber to Michels, 1908, quoted in Mommsen, 1974, p. 87). The crucial feature of the state is located within its role as the major authoritative association within a given territory. For the state to maintain its central position it has to claim a monopoly of the legitimate use of force. Domination, or as Weber termed it, 'the authoritarian power of command' (Roth, 1978, p. 946) is a necessary and inevitable feature of this process. State domination requires:

- a minimum of voluntary compliance;
- an acceptance of commands as valid norms; and
- a belief in the legitimacy of the form of domination.

Hence, force, although always present, is not enough to ensure the stability and survival of a regime; all systems have to provide a source of legitimation for their form of governance.

Weber suggested three types of legitimate domination. The first, 'traditional', rests on a belief in the 'sanctity of immemorial custom'. The second, 'charismatic', centres on a devotion to the exceptional sanctity of heroism or exemplary character of an individual person. The final type, 'rational', focuses on a conviction as to the legality of enacted rules (Runciman, 1978, pp. 226-50). It is important to note that these three pure types did not represent historical stages. Any empirical situation could involve elements of any of the three, in different combinations. How do these ideal types of legitimate domination relate to different institutionalised state forms?

'Traditional' domination centred oh patrimonial states and feudalism; 'charismatic' domination was an inherently unstable form caused by what Weber termed 'the routinisation of charisma'; and 'rational' domination was seen as the major state form in Western societies. Weber (Roth, 1968, p. 1117) argued that charismatic domination was the 'creative revolutionary force of history', but that it was the fate of charisma to decline with the development of permanent institutional structures.

Bureaucracy was viewed by Weber as the epitome of a formally-organised structure based on rational principles. However, he also believed that bureaucracy first arose in patrimonial states and, as such, lacked certain features deemed to be essential to modern democracies.

Rational Bureaucracy Involves:

- the organisation of functions on a continuous and regulated basis;
- a functional division of spheres of competence;
- hierarchical organisation with control of higher over lower levels;
- working rules which may be technical, or norms requiring training;
- officials who are separated from the ownership of the means of production or administration;
- officials who cannot appropriate their office;
- administration which involves a written record; and a bureaucratic administrative staff.

Hence, there exists a hierarchy of domination which contains a system of rationally consistent rules and job specialisation among the officials, who administer the rules in a highly impersonal way.

As Weber puts it:

> The development of modern organisational forms in all spheres (state, church, army, party, economy, interest groups, voluntary associations, charitable bodies etc.) is simply identical with the development and continuous increase of bureaucratic administration. (Roth and Wittich, 1968, p. 223)

Weber was a liberal who thought that politics inevitably involved an unceasing struggle for power, and that nation state interests should supersede all others. At the same time, he was clearly a liberal in anguish (see Momsen, 1974, p. 95) who argued that the central issue was not that there was too much freedom, too much individualism or too much democracy. He was concerned with establishing how one could preserve any individual freedom.

How is it possible to check and control the power of state bureaucracy? As Weber puzzles, 'How will democracy even in this limited sense be at all possible?' (Roth and Wittich, 1968, p. 1403) Here, he broadens the scope of his critique of liberal democracy and power relations from one which focused on the relationship between, and contradictions of, democracy and capitalism, to one which emphasises the role of the state in securing elite domination. Schumpeter's approach involved a mixture of competing methodologies; a tool-bag of Weberian, utilitarian and Marxist method. He shared Marx's view of the inevitability of the collapse of the capitalist state under the weight of its own contradictions and, like Marx, argued that large corporations dominated the production and distribution of goods.

Despite this, Schumpeter was a reluctant socialist who rejected Marxist class analysis and class conflict.

As David Held observes, for Schumpeter:

> the definitive element of socialism was the planning of resources: an institutional pattern which allowed a central authority control over the production system. Interpreted in this manner, socialism was not necessarily incompatible, as Weber had asserted, with democracy. (Held, 1987, p. 169)

Remarkably for Schumpeter, the most important task for socialists was to develop the most appropriate model of democracy to meet the demands of 'big government.' Here, he highlighted the importance of the planning of resources in economic and political life. In particular, he emphasised the need to re-examine the role of both bureaucratisation and democrarisation in providing the conditions for a centralised governing tradition. It was within this context that he embraced the need for a leadership model of democracy) He rejected explicitly what he perceived to be the classical doctrine of democracy, and was a vociferous advocate of the leadership state. Because, in Schumpeter's view, 'the people' are, and can be, nothing more than 'producers of governments', a mechanism to select 'the men who are able to do the deciding' (Schumpeter, 1976, p. 296).

Hence he refuted the notion of the 'popular will' as a social construct that had no rational basis, as a 'manufactured' rather than a genuine popular will. 'Popular will' is therefore the 'product and not the motive power for the political process'. Within this formulation, democracy and socialism can only be compatible as a form of "competitive elitism', and if the conditions for its successful functioning are met (Held, 1987, p. 177). Schumpeter's theory of democracy reflected support for competitive parry systems in which democracy merely served as a source of legitimation for the governing elite.; He quite clearly failed to recognise that, rather than safeguarding the last remnants of individual liberty, the competitive party system merely enabled political elites to manipulate and distort the political will of the citizen.

As Macpherson (1977, p. 89) observes, Schumpeter appeared to confuse a 'competitive' political system with an oligopolistic one, in which:

> there are only a few sellers, a few suppliers of political goods . . . Where there are so few sellers, they need not and do not respond to the buyers demands as they must do in a fully competitive system. They can set prices and set the range of goods that will be offered. More than that, they can, to a considerable extent create [their own] demand.

Following Weber, the democratic elitist model developed a broad view of the state. The state has both capacity and autonomy as a regulator and distorter of markets. The democratic elitist model also emphasises the unattainability of classical participatory democratic forms of political organisation. Joseph Schumpeter's 'equilibrium model' develops this theme, arguing that a division of labour between political activists and a passive electorate was crucial for strong, efficient government and the defence of liberty. Schumpeter accepts the inevitability of hierarchy, observing the democratic process as a forum for legitimate elite Competition: 'it is simply an institutional arrangement for reaching Political decisions not an end in itself (Schumpeter, 1976, p. 126). It is not surprising that Schumpeter's conclusion should claim that: 'dictatorships might better serve the popular interest than democracies'. Political elites are thus both inevitable and necessary.

3. Modern Elitist Perspectives

(a) National Elite Power Network Studies

The study of national elite power networks (NEPNs) has long been a focus of study in the USA and the UK. The key concern of this literature has been to identify the degree to which national elite structures are unified or diversified. The origins of these studies lie in the pluralist-radical elitist debates of the 1940s and 1950s in the USA. These had two chief protagonists: C.Wright Mills (1956) who in *The Power Elite* provided an account of the role of power elites within the US Executive; and Walter Burnham who, in *The Managerial Revolution,* argued that a new managerial elite was in the process of establishing control across all capitalist states. However, it was the work of the radical elitist C. Wright Mills that had the most impact on future NEPNs.

Mills' theory involved a three level gradation of the distribution of power. At the top level were those in command of the major institutional hierarchies of modern society - the executive branch of the national government, the large business corporations, and the military establishment. The pluralist model of competing interests, Mills argued, applied only to the 'middle levels', the semi-organised interaction between interest group and legislative politics which pluralists mistook for the entire power structure of the capitalist stated.

A politically fragmented 'society of the masses' occupied the bottom level. Mills' (1956, pp. 167-9) work suggested a close relationship between economic elites and governmental elites: the 'corporate rich' and the 'political directorate'. He maintained that the growing centralisation of power in the federal executive branch of government had been accompanied by a declining role for professional politicians and a growing role for 'political outsiders' from the corporate world (ibid., p. 235). Despite this. Mills contended that it would be a mistake 'to believe that the political apparatus is merely an extension of the corporate world, or that it had been taken over by the representatives of the corporate rich' (ibid., p. 170).

Here, Mills wanted to distinguish his position from what he termed the 'simple Marxian view', which held that economic elites were the the real holders of power. For this reason, he used the term 'power elite' rather than 'ruling class', a term which for him implied too much economic determinism (ibid., pp. 276-7). Crucial Mills argued that political, military and economic elites all exercised a considerable degree of autonomy, were often in conflict, and rarely acted in concert. *The Power Elite* provided the most important critique of pluralism written from an elitist perspective. It emphasised that far from being an independent arbiter of the national interest, the state was actually dominated by a NEPN of politicians, military and corporate bosses who moulded public policy to suit their own ends. Mills' analysis was given an empirical fillip by a series of 'community power' studies which demonstrated the validity of the elitist interpretation of American politics. In the debate that ensued throughout the 1950s and 1960s, pluralists emphasised the mistaken nature of the claims of the community power theorists (see Chapter 11). NEPN theorists in the USA such as Mills and Domhoff found a considerable amount of elite integration, although with various bases in the national power structure. According to Mills (1956, p. 292):

> The conception of the power elite and of its unity rests upon the corresponding developments and the coincidence of interests among economic, political, and military organisations. It also rests upon the similarity of origins and outlook, and the social and personal intermingling of the top circles from each of these dominant hierarchies.

The existence of a broad, inclusive network of powerful people with similar social origins, in different institutions, is an important feature of this view of the power structure. However, the NEPN literature identifies three key dimensions of political elite integration:

(i) Social homogeneity (Mills, 1956; Domhoff, 1967) which emphasises shared class and status origins.

(ii) Value consensus (Prewitt and Stone, 1973), focusing on agreement among elites on the 'rules of the game'; and,

(iii) Personal interaction among elites, both informally through social and personal interaction and formally through membership of common organisations.

Further, the third dimension is reflected in the interlocking directorates of major US corporations. These ties are seen to foster integration, cohesiveness and consensus within the business community. Many social scientists, particularly in the USA, have examined the sociometric ties among elites in individual communities.

Notably the UK, NEPNs have rarely reached any degree of sophistication. A number of historians have considered the fate of the English aristocracy (for example, Winchester, 1981) dwelling on the changing nature of the relationship between landed and mercantile interests. William Guttsman (1963) analysed the decline of the upper class and the rise of the middle class as a principal source of elite renewal. Anthony Sampson (for example, Sampson, 1982), in his exhaustive accounts of the anatomy of Britain, has argued that the aristocracy no longer rules and, indeed, that there is no longer a real social elite at all.

Further, Sampson contends that the various hierarchies of British society have become gradually more open in their recruitment, and the diversity of these hierarchies is such that there is no single centre of power.

Corporate Power Debates

The aim of this sub-section is to provide a simple overview of the central considerations within elitist thought on the analysis of the relationship between business elites and government. This is a particularly fertile area of analysis as it provides a further example of convergence between competing theories of the stare that is crystallised in the 'structural approach' to the study of corporate power; an approach that is implicit both in the work of Charles Lindblom (1977, 1982) and in neo-Marxist analyses of the liberal-democratic stare (Marsh, 1983). These debates focus primarily upon the relationship between economic power and political power as it is exerted through the modern interventionist state. The ensuing discussion will argue that, first, the neo-pluralist position has more in common with elitism than pluralism; and, second, that the corporate power debate in the USA provides a major source of convergence between revisionist pluralist, elitist and Marxist theories of the stare. Neo-pluralism, is a critical theory which may be identified with the work of Charles Lindblom (1977, 1982).

It rests on the structuralist view that because of the dependency of Western democracies on capitalist economies, the disproportionate influence of business corporations over the state is an inevitable structural necessity, 'for the state to operate in conditions of stability, and therefore of political equilibrium — business needs must first be met', Lindblom criticises liberal democratic theory for failing to take into account the 'privileged position of business'. Lindblom's work has not gone without criticism. Whiie many pluralists have modified their methodology to cope with these critiques of corporate power, and have reconsidered aspects of democratic theory, a number of political scientists, who may be viewed as methodological pluralists, have dissented from the new conventional wisdom.

Vogel criticises Lindblom's position on the basis that it exaggerates the role that investment decisions play in the performance of the economy. Moreover, he suggests that Lindblom 'underestimates the options available to politicians to manipulate business decisions and fails to appreciate that businessmen are not unique in requiring inducements to perform their social role' (Vogel, 1987, p. 385). This leads Vogel to the conclusion the while corporations undeniably exercise significant political power, the scope and magnitude may be accounted for within a pluralist framework of interest group politics:

> My contention is not that individual companies, trade associations and interindustry coalitions do not weild significant political power, of course they do. It is rather that we do not require a distinctive methodology for measuring the political power of business in capitalist democracies. Business is not unique. There is nothing about the nature, scope or magnitude of the power wielded by business that cannot be accounted for within the framework of a sophisticated model of interest-group politics. (Vogel, 1987, p. 408)

Lindblom is also held to be culpable for his failure to analyse the divisions within business, to recognise the power potentialities of other groups, or to take into account the flexibility involved in the relationship between business and the state (see Marsh, 1983).

In contrast to neo-pluralists, neo-conservative political scientists consider corporate political power to be on the decline (see Steinfel, 1979). Jeanne Kirkpatrick (1979), for example, identifies the emergence of a new class, a knowledge elite that threatens the political aspirations of corporate power. Kirkpatrick argues that this new class has been in the forefront of efforts to shift various responsibilities from the private sector to the government, and has had a significant role in developing public policies hostile to business and the market system (Kirkpatrick, 1979, p. 46).

Aaron Wildavsky, on the other hand, has defended the corporation as a bulwark of pluralism and a sanctuary for private life against the bureaucratic power of the state (Wildavsky, 1978, p. 234). James Wilson (1973) uses a tool bag approach in assessing competing theories of political power (Marxist, elitist, bureaucratic and pluralist). Wilson concludes that no single model provides an accurate description of the political system as a whole, and that different models are applicable in different policy areas. None the less, Wilson may still be considered to be a pluralist because while some groups are able to dominate particular areas, their power is not necessarily transferable to other policy areas or to the overall structure of power. The structural dimension of corporate power implicit in the work of revisonist pluralists such as Lindblom (1982) has important implications for democratic theory and pluralism. It places decision making firmly within an elitist context, or what Lindblom has termed the 'imprisoned zone of decision making' (1982, p. 324).

This suggests a very strong form of elite domination that does not fit happily with democratic theory. Once again, the pluralist response represents a remarkable retreat from the classical position. It is recognised that power is open to competition between numerous groups, but political participation is circumscribed by unequal access to both resources and the decision-making process.

Further, multiple groups exist, but a corporate bias predominates. However, in their view, the integrity of the pluralist position is maintained because no one group dominates all policy networks. In both the above cases, the paradigmatic shift within pluralism towards the elitist and Marxist position is striking.

Corporatism and Beo-corporatism

Corporatism emerged as a strand of Catholic social doctrine that was adapted and subsequently modified (some would say vulgarised) in the authoritarian regimes of Benito Mussolini's Italy (1922-43) and Antonio Salazar's Portugal

(1933-74). It was later resurrected in several European democracies under the name of 'neo-corporatism'. Like many such concepts in social science, different people have used it to mean different things, but Philippe Schmitter (1974, pp. 93—4) provides the most exact conceptual definition:

> Corporatism can be defined as a system of interest representation in which the constituent units are organized into a limited number of singular, compulsory, noncompetitive, hierarchically ordered and functionally differentiated categories, recognised or licensed (if not created) by the state and granted a deliberate representational monopoly within their respective categories in exchange for observing certain controls on their selection of leaders and articulation of demands and supports.

Hence, corporatism is a model of state-group intermediation in which the interests of the state and certain private sector interests fuse. These interests (principally large firms, but also to some extent organised labour and other private interests such as the professions) enter into negotiations and compromise with government agreeing to certain concessions and undertaking certain functions of governments In mm, the government supports them financially and forwards their interests in policy-making.

Corporatist theory received an enormous boost in Britain during the period of the 1974-79 Labour governments, when initiatives such as planning agreements, incomes policies and the National Enterprise Board (NEB) seemed to indicate a move towards a system of private ownership coupled with state direction. Corporatism is therefore best understood as an ideal state form which represents a fusion of state and private sector interests (Cox, 1988). Elites emerge within this context of social partnership because of the need for governments to increase Gross Domestic Product (GDP) in order to stay in power.

Hence, sectional interests almost inevitably become uniquely privileged within policy-making. The most distinctive feature of corporatist theory lies in few structures of elite domination. An institutional setting for legitimate elite domination is created in which elite circulation is dependent upon the bargaining resources of the various sectional interests.

Corporatists have observed a general downgrading of liberal democrate and pluralist forms of state group intermediation (Schmitter Lehmbruch, 1979). As such, corporatism represented a critique of both pluralist and socialist ideal-typical political forms.

However, Corporatism was very much a product of its time, and while Schmitter (1979, p. 38) did provide some empirical evidence to suggest that Brazil, Spain, Portugal Greece, Austria, Italy and Germany all had forms of state-group intermediation approximating the corporatist model, it remained equally possible to provide examples to the Neo-corporatism emerged in the wake of a wave of pluralist critiques of Corporatist methodology (see for example, Cawson, 1985). They contended that there was nothing within corporatist method which had not already been accounted for in revisionist and methodological currents of neo-pluralism.

Corporatism was also criticised by Marxists, who argued that it ignored the ideological dimension of analysis and granted unwarranted autonomy to the state in mediating between complete sectional interests. The neo-corporarists reshaped their argument accordingly. It is apt to quote Cox (1988, p. 297) who observes:

> Instead of accepting that the concept might not be as widely applicable as they first thought, to save its integrity they redefined it so that its meaning subtly shifted from being a descriptive concept about an ideal-typical political form of the state to become a catch-all phrase for special interests bargaining with the state.

In fact, they argued that, as hierarchies develop in all associational forms, corporatism could be used as a concept for understanding policy-making Neo-corporatists identify the existence of monopolies of sectional interests within the policy-making process. This is reflected in closed policy networks, but not necessarily tripartite ones. Within this formulation, elite circulation is still dependent upon the bargaining resources of the sectional interests involved. Whether or not the corporatist state form ever existed is still open to -much debate.

Many of the claims made in the literature are certainly stronger on assertion than on evidence and remain vulnerable to the Marxist charge that they fail to specify whose interest this new bargained corporatism serves. In sum, it still provides a poor understanding of how and why policy networks operate in the fundamentally elitist way that they do. In this sense, corporatism and "co-corporatism provide insufficient methodological tools for analysing power monopolies within policy networks.

To sum up, this chapter has made two central arguments. First, elitism still provides an important focus for the work of political scientists and political sociologists, particularly in the USA, and has presented a compelling critique of the liberal democratic model. Second, when contrasted with other theories of the state, the elitist position appears to be both theoretically unsophisticated and conceptually underdeveloped. There are four central reasons for this. First, despite a large number of empirical studies, many of which have been cited in this chapter, elite theory remains difficult to sustain in an empirical sense. Second, as Birch (1993, p. 202) reminds us, 'there is no adequate and convincing theory showing that democratic systems must always be elitist in practice'. Third, elite theory offers an insufficient conceptualisation of the relationship between elite circulation and the nature of state crisis and legitimation Fourth, elite theory offers a limited account of the structure of elite networks, both within the nation state, between centre and region, and outside the nation state, between nations. Yet, despite this, elite theory still contributes much to the tool bag of the political scientist.

Thus, the argument about the American power structure is as much philosophic as it is empirical. While the debate continues, however, we should continue to remind ourselves that members of an upper class making up less than 1 per cent of the population own 20 to 25 per cent of all privately held wealth and 45 to 50 per cent of all privately held corporate stock; they are overrepresented in seats of formal power from the corporation to the federal government; and they win much more often than they lose on issues ranging from the tax structure to labor law to foreign policy.

The future of elite theory continues to look bright, because there is now a distinct global dimension to the discourse, of the kind suggested by David Held's conception of global interconnectedness (Held, 1991)) His view may be summed up as a rejection of the underlying premises of democratic theory that democracies should be treated as: self-contained units; that democracies are clearly demarcated on demarcated one from another that change within democracies can be understood largely with reference to the internal structures and dynamics of national democratic politics; and that democratic politics is itself ultimately an expression of the interplay between forces operating within the nation-state, (ibid., p. 199)

As such the growing integration of economics, technology, communications and law, together with the transnational character of capital, has eroded nation state sovereignty of the kind jealously guarded in the British context, and undermined state capacities. The density of current global politics and its impact upon state theorising has been dramatic.

As McGrew (1992, p. 12) comments:

> It encompasses not just political relations between states, and relations between states and international organisations, but also a vast array of transnational interactions which cut across national societies, as well as transgovernmental relations which permeate the institutional structures of the state itself.

Elitists hive a new, fertile ground for analysis that will inevitably entail confronting an important source of weakness in the elitist approach: its national specificity.

While the credibility of the elitist approach increased in response to the dramatic rise in the size and complexity of the capitalist state, its future development is likely to reflect a concern with the emergence of new social and political forms as a consequence of globalisation pressures. Analysing how far increased globalisation has facilitated changes in state form must be a key concern for contemporary elitists.

As is obvious from the above discussion the aristocratic version of this theory is the Classic Elite Theory which is based on two ideas:

1. power lies in position of authority in key economic and political institutions
2. the psychological difference that sets Elites apart is that they have personal resources, for instance intelligence and skills, and a vested interest in the government; while the rest are incompetent and do not have the capabilities of governing themselves, the elite are resourceful and will strive to make the government to work. For in reality, the elite have the most to lose in a failed government.

Classical Elite Theorists

Vilfredo Pareto

Pareto emphasized the psychological and intellectual superiority that the Elites obtained, he believed that the elites were the highest accomplishers in any field and he discussed how there were two types of Elites:

1. governing elites;
2. non-governing elites.

He also extended on the idea that a whole elite can be replaced by a new one and how one can circulate from being elite to nonelite.

Gaetano Mosca

Mosca emphasized on the sociological and personal characteristics of elites, he said they were an organized minority and how masses are the unorganized majority. The ruling class is composed of the ruling Elite and the sub-Elites. He divided the world into two groups

1. ruling class;
2. class that is ruled.

Elites have intellectual, moral, and material superiority that is highly esteemed and influential.

Robert Michels

The sociologist Michels developed the Iron Law of Oligarchy where social and political organizations are run by few individuals, he said that social organization is key as well as the division of labor so elites were the ones that ruled. He believed that all organizations were elitist and that elites have three basic principles that help in the bureaucratic structure of political organization

1. need for leaders, specialized staff and facilities;
2. utilization of facilities by leaders within their organization;
3. the importance of the psychological attributes of the leaders.

Other Notable Elite Theorists

C. Wright Mills

Mills published his book *The Power Elite* in 1956, claiming a new sociological perspective on systems of power in the United States. He identified a triumvirate of power groups – political, economic and military – which form a distinguishable, although not unified, power wielding body in the American state.

Mills proposed that this group had been generated through a process of rationalisation at work in all advanced industrial societies whereby the mechanisms of power became concentrated funnelling overall control into the hands of a limited, somewhat corrupt group. This reflected a decline in politics as an arena for debate and relegation to a merely formal level of discourse. This macro-scale analysis sought to point out the degradation of democracy in "advanced" societies and the fact that power generally lies outside the boundaries of elected representatives. A main influence for the study was Franz Leopold Neumanns book, Behemoth: The Structure and Practice of National Socialism in 1942, a study of how Nazism came to power in a democratic state like Germany. It provided the tools to analyse the entire total structure of a political system and served as a warning of what could happen in a modern capitalistic democracy.

Floyd Hunter

The elite theory analysis of power was also applied on the micro scale in community power studies such as that by Floyd Hunter (1953). Hunter examined in detail the power relationships evident in his "Regional City" looking for the "real" holders of power rather than those in obvious official positions. He posited a structural-functional approach which mapped the hierarchies and webs of interconnection operating within the city – mapping relationships of power between businessmen, politicians, clergy etc. The study was promoted to debunk current concepts of any 'democracy' present within urban politics and reaffirm the arguments for a true representative democracy.

This type of analysis was also used in later, larger scale, studies such as that carried out by M. Schwartz examining the power structures within the sphere of the corporate elite in the USA.

G. William Domhoff

In his controversial book "Who Rules America?", G. William Domhoff researched the power structure in the United states. He claims (agreeing mostly with Hunters work) that an elite class that owns and manages large income-producing properties (like banks and corporations) dominate the American power structure politically and economically.

Domhoff researched the local as well as national decision making processes.

James Burnham

Burnham's early work *The Managerial Revolution* sought to express the movement of all functional power into the hands of managers rather than politicians or businessmen – separating ownership and control. Many of these ideas were adapted by paleoconservatives Samuel T. Francis and Paul Gottfried in their theories of the managerial state.

Robert D. Putnam

Putnam saw the development of technical and exclusive knowledge among administrators and other specialist groups as a mechanism by which power is stripped from the democratic process and slipped sideways to the advisors and specialists influencing the decision making process.

> "If the dominant figures of the past hundred years have been the entrepreneur, the businessman, and the industrial executive, the 'new men' are the scientists, the mathematicians, the economists, and the engineers of the new intellectual technology."

Thomas R. Dye

Dye in his book *Top Down Policymaking,* argues that U.S. public policy does not result from the "demands of the people," but rather from Elite consensus found in Washington, D.C. based non-profit foundations, think tanks, special-interest groups, and promient lobbyists and law firms.

3

Pluralism

> "There are multiple centres of power, none of which is wholly sovereign."
>
> —*Dahl*

First it is remarkable that the 'Pluralism' as a theory is an enigma. Despite being the dominant theory in political science, it is remarkably undertheorised. Consequently, there are many different interpretations of pluralism. It is at the same time normative, prescriptive and descriptive. It is normative in that pluralism is seen as the best form of government; it is prescriptive in providing a model of what all governments ideally should be; and it is descriptive in its analysis of government.

This under-theorisation and confusion of ends makes it very difficult to define pluralism. Frequently, there have been attempts to characterise pluralism, crudely, as a belief that the state is neutral; that societal groups are potentially equal in their influence, and that access to the political system is open. However, as Paul Hirst points out, one of the most prominent pluralists, Robert Dahl argued that pluralism 'does *not* mean that *all* the citizens are included in the political process. Dahl makes it evident and emphasises the fact that many citizens are inactive, that income and wealth and political resources are unequally distributed'.

Here in this chapter we intend to provide a clarification of the main features of pluralism. It will demonstrate the way in which much mainstream political science literature has been at least implicitly influenced by pluralism. We will highlight some of the problems of pluralism and will look at how it has developed as a result of criticism. Finally, we will examine the resurgence of interest in pluralism from contemporary radical political theory.

Salient Features of Pluralism

It is pertinent to note that the key feature of pluralism is difference or diversity. The complexity of the modem liberal state means that no single group, class or organisation can dominate society. Pluralism sees a separation between the stare and civil society; a difference between economic and political power; and a variation in the interests that are successful in particular policy areas.

Power is non-cumulative and dispersed. Hence the role of the state is to regulate conflicts in society rather than to dominate society in pursuit of particular interests. Pluralists have an underdeveloped theory of the state. The notion of the state assumes an all-encompassing authoritative organisation chat governs society.

Pluralists are wary of using a concept which they see as too broad and talk of the government rather than the state. Consequently, the pluralist notion of 'the state' is of a set of institutions such as the executive, legislature, civil service and judiciary that are distinct from civil society. Through the mechanisms of elections and pressure politics the government is reflective of society's demands and constrained by the countervailing powers of civil society and other organisations.

Even within the state there are numerous constraints on other State actors. So, for example, there are constraints on the executive from the legislature and judiciary. More importantly, there are constraints within government from other departments. Pluralists do not deny that there is a tendency for certain groups to establish close relationships with particular departments or agencies. One of the principal theorists of pluralism, David Truman, acknowledged that 'institutionalised relationships between an agency and its attendant interest groups' could develop (Truman, 1951, p. 10) and this could lead to other interests being ignored. However, Wilson maintains that there is 'Whitehall pluralism'.

Even if one department disregards the interests of a particular group, their views are represented 'by the fact that other departments have checks and have different departmental views correspondingly'. The Ministry of Agriculture may be very close to the farmers and attempt to allow the fanners' interests to dominate agricultural policy, bur the Department of Trade and Industry will ensure that trade issues are considered; the Department of Environment will press for environmental interests to be considered; and the Treasury will act so that tax payers do not have to subsidise fanners too much. For pluralists, the state is often seen as a site of conflict between departments that represent a range of interest groups. Authority is dispersed even within the government (Eckstein, 1963, p. 392) and hence no single interest is able to dominate the state.

Yet, the state is rarely neutral but reflects the range of group pressures it faces. Easton (1967, p. 172) believes that 'policy arises from the interaction of various social elements'. The process of making policy within the state is an attempt to bargain between a range of conflicting interests. Politics is a constant process of negotiation that ensures conflicts are resolved peacefully.

Basically, the politics as the resolution of conflicting means that groups are a of politics is the analysis of groups. The policy process is essentially a continual process of conflict and exchange between different groups, with the government being classified as just another group:

> All phenomena of government are phenomena of groups pressing one another, forming one another, and pushing our new groups and group representation (the organs or agencies of government) to mediate adjustments. It is only as we isolate these group activities, determine their representative values, and get the whole process stated in terms of them, that we approach to a satisfactory knowledge of government. (Bentley, 1967, p. 269)

Notably, is by organising into groups that individuals can represent their interests to government. Pluralists define the state as a discrete organisation making policy in response to the myriad of groups pressing on the government. Consequently, there are a vast array of pluralist pressure group studies that examine the methods and success of pressure groups. Pluralists do not see all pressure groups as having equal resources, access or influence. For instance, pluralists acknowledge that business is in a privileged position.

Dahl recognised that 'the goals of businessmen are legitimised by a system of beliefs widely shared throughout the community'. For Finer, the importance of economic interests to the economy meant that 'their cooperation must be won, rather than their services commanded. They do not direct but they may veto'. Yet there are a range of constraints on economic groups. First, economic groups are only interested in a limited-range of issues and thus do not try to influence the majority of policies.

Second, economic groups do not have snared interests and are as likely to be in conflict with each other as to be in a coalition to defeat the less economically dominant. Third, the existence of one powerful group is likely to lead to the development of a countervailing power that will act as a constraint (Galbraith, 1963, p. 125). The creation of a business association will, for instance, lead to the establishment of a countervailing trade union. Fourth, although Dahl (1961, p. 228) acknowledged inequality in the distribution of resources for influencing political outcomes, he also realised that there were a range of different resources available for influencing public officials and that, 'Individuals best off in their access to one kind of resource are often badly off with respect to many other resources'. In other words, if a group is well resourced in terms of finance it is likely to have limited resources in terms of votes.

As Finer (1966, p. 118) argued:

> The comparative strength of rich associations is an argument which does not impress me; partly because the uses to which this wealth can be put are so circumscribed, partly because there are such effective ways for poor associations to influence public policy, and partly because the capacity of publicity to mould political attitudes is so highly problematical.

Notably, rich groups might have very close contacts with senior ministers, but poor associations can use the media and campaigns to attract attention and influence policy. Consequently, resources are dispersed, admittedly unequally, between a range of groups and elites, and it is impossible for a single class or interest to dominate society. Fifth, Truman claims the government takes account of the interests of 'unorganised and potential groups' and, therefore, they do not need 'organised expression except when these needs are flagrantly violated'.

Government is prepared to take account of groups that are unorganised either in order to ensure that they do not become organised - a kind of 'anticipated reaction' - or because the government is highly motivated by the need to win an election (Beer, 1982). Politicians are therefore driven to act in the interest of the electorate rather than for organised groups. Finer believed that it is the duty of government to take account of the counter-claims of interests whether or not they are represented, concluding 'on the whole it does work' (Finer, 1966, p. 128).

Although certain groups are advantaged in terms of resources and access, the pressure group system as a whole, and the nature of the state, ensures that there are checks on potentially powerful groups. Despite the recognition that conflict between groups is endemic within liberal democracy, this conflict rarely threatens to undermine political stability. The political system as a whole is maintained by a consensus which defines the limits of political actions and the framework of policy outcomes.

Dahl maintains that although severe business/labour conflicts frequently occurred in the USA, these never threatened the political and economic system. An ideology that promoted wide support for democracy and capitalism was accepted because of the absence of a socialist party; the fact that coalitions were often conglomerates; the level of economic growth; the absence of a high degree of class differentiation; and because workers never became a majority of the population (Dahl, 1967, pp. 439-40).

Almond and Verba (1963, p. 491), in their study of political culture in five nations, maintained that: 'If there is no consensus within society, there can be little potentiality for the peaceful resolution of policy differences that is associated with the democratic process.' For democratic society to work effectively there has to be a degree of consensus concerning the fundamental values of a society shared by the competing groups. The importance of consensus to the pluralist conception of society underpins the pluralist notion of power. Power for Polsby (1963, p. 5) is the capacity of one actor to do something affecting another actor, which changes the probable pattern of specified future events'. Or for Dahl, '*A* has power over *B to* the extent that he can get *B* to do something that *B* the pluralist approach are: Who is involved in the decision-making process; and who was successful in getting their preferences accepted as decisions? Who was it who could be *seen to* influence outcomes? According to N. Polsby, 'The researcher should study actual behaviour, either from first hand or by reconstructing behaviour from documents, informants, newspapers and other appropriate sources'.

Notably, pluralist conception of power dictates pluralist methodology. Pluralists examine observable behaviour and observable outcomes. Hewitt (1974) highlighted the nature of pluralist methodology when he studied national decision-making in Britain. He focused on a number of issues within the following policy areas: foreign affairs, economic policy, welfare policy and social policy. He then analysed which groups were involved in each issue area and discovered that, 'Very few organisations were involved "significantly" in more than one issue'. Hewitt concluded:

> From the evidence presented, it is clear that policy making does not appear to be elitist in the sense that any single elite interest is dominant. Instead the picture of national power that is revealed suggests a 'pluralist' interpretation since a diversity of conflicting interests are involved in many issues, without any one interest being consistently successful in realising its own goals. (Hewitt, 1974, p. 61)

Pluralists focus on who does what, and who is successful in achieving his/ her goals.

Advantage of This Approach

1. It does not assume anything about the distribution of power (Polsby, 1960):
2. It is possible to determine empirically who does or does not have power. By omitting concepts such as false consciousness, dominant ideology and hegemony, pluralists develop a theory of power that is testable empirically.
3. By developing a notion of modern society and polity as fragmented, diverse and democratic, they provide a more accurate description of the distribution of power than do monolithic Marxist or elitist theories.

Pluralism provides an intuitively plausible account of the policy-making process in modern liberal democratic societies. It points to the fragmentation of both society and the state. Modem society is divided into a variety of groups with different interests and a range of resources. These groups use their resources to influence a diverse polity with its own conflicts and divisions. The complexity of the state, society and the policy process means that it is impossible for a single group or class to dominate. In order for a democratic society to survive there has to be accommodation by the state of the various societal groups.

There are a number of problems with the pluralist

analysis of the policy process and state—group relationships. This section will examine some of the internal inconsistencies of pluralism and examine the criticisms of pluralism from alternative theoretical traditions. Pluralism is far more subtle and complex than many of its critics have suggested. Pluralists are aware of inequalities in society, and between groups, and recognise that through institutionalised relationships some groups have privileged access to the government.

However, despite this sophistication, pluralism still sees power as being widely dispersed and non-cumulative — success in one policy area does not increase power in other policy areas. It also maintains that there is no connection between economic and political power. Consequently, pluralists maintain a benign view of the political system which leads them to overestimate the ease of access to the policy process. Pluralists suggest that if groups do not have access, it is because they have not tried assiduously, or that their interests have not been sufficiently threatened. They deny that it is possible to exclude groups for a long period. However, there are a range of empirical studies which demonstrate the exclusion of groups from agriculture (Smith, 1990a); nuclear policy and prison reform.

Pluralists do not take adequate account of the mechanisms that exist within the policy process for the exclusion of undesirable groups. For example, for groups to be represented on a government advisory committee they have to be seen to be legitimate. This means that they have to conform to the 'rules of the game', which involves behaving in certain ways and accepting particular views and values. These views and values conform to the interests of the dominant groups in the policy process. For example, the group 'Radical Alternatives to Prison' were not given access to prison policy because their policy goal was radical alternatives to the prison system (Ryan, 1978).

Remarkably, this notion of the ease of access to the political process is related to problems with pluralist methodology. Because pluralists are concerned with observable behaviour, they see evidence of consultation as an indicator of access, and therefore influence.

If A supports a policy Z, and the government consults A and chooses policy Z, A is seen to be influential. However, all that is demonstrated is a correlation between consultation with A and outcome Z. The relationship might not be causal. By focusing on the observable, pluralists may miss the real reasons for policy. They do not examine the ideological and structural context within which policy is made (Smith, 1990b). The influence of pressure groups does not derive from their resources bur also from the institutional, historical and ideological context within which decisions ate made. This context biases the decision-making process so that certain interests are privileged over others. For example, teachers' unions Rave always been in daily contact with officials at the Department for Education. This is a degree of access unavailable to other groups in education. Similarly, groups that share the ideology of dominant actors are much more likely to gain access.

To grasp the influence of groups it is important to assess the historical development of a policy area, to examine how groups became involved, what pressure groups were excluded and what policy-making institutions developed. Pluralists fail to recognise, because of their positivist method, the role of ideas in shaping policy outcomes. In other words, they concentrate on observable behaviour and thus are unable to evaluate how ideology may shape the actions of policy-makers. This failure to understand ideology leads to the assumption that society is underpinned by a consensus of values. Moreover, this consensus is seen as being politically neutral and the result of shared interests. However, the degree of consensus is in itself questionable and even where consensus does exist, it is not neutral but serves a particular set of interests. Dahl points out that the acceptance of the market capitalism is part of the consensus in the USA.

Dahl even states that:

> Fortunately for the politicians it is easy to avoid the hostility of the (economic and social) notables, for living conditions and the belief system has not—at least so far—generated demands for local policies markedly antagonistic to the goals of businessmen and notables. (Dahl, 1961, p. 84)

It is also questionable whether countervailing powers are as important as pluralists assume. Is it really the case that consumer groups provide a constraint on the power of producers? Consider the situation of consumers and producers in relation to the Thatcher and Major Governments.

The Conservative governments have been influenced by New Right ideology and committed to the extension of the market. Consequently, consumer policy has shifted from one of consumer protection to one of improving the market choice of consumers. The Thatcher Government set up a deregulation unit, abolished the Department of Prices and Consumer Protection, and attempted to lessen the impact of EC (now EU) consumer legislation (Smith, 1993).

With a *laissez-faire* ideology and a stated goal of

increasing the competitiveness and profitability of industry, can it be maintained that the government gave similar consideration to the interests of consumers and producers? Pluralists may accept the weakness of consumer groups, but would see consumer interests being protected through 'Whitehall pluralism'. However, the concept of Whitehall pluralism is questionable. On many occasions, other departments will not have the opportunity to represent alternative interests. In most instances, policy is made within departments without reference to Cabinet or Cabinet committees (Smith *et al.,* 1993).

Even when policy is referred to interdepartmental committees, the extent to which other departments will represent alternative interests is limited. It is usually the case chat ministers are too busy to read the papers of other departments in order to offer constructive alternatives. They are also wary of criticising colleagues when they may want these colleagues' support for their own department's policy.

Besides this, it is doubtful that potential groups exercise much influence over decision-makers. Departments do not represent their interests, not least because it must be difficult to recognise these interests. Moreover, it is unlikely that potential groups offer much of an electoral threat. It is rare in the UK for a single issue to sway large numbers of voters, and the members of potential groups are likely to have many conflicting interests. If a politician appeals to one potential group, he or she could lose the votes of another. It is also the case that most potential groups have great difficulty in organising.

Consumers and the elderly do not meet collectively; they lack resources; they often have conflicting interests; and they have very little, and diffuse, economic power. The threat to their interests has to be extremely great for them to organise into actual groups. Indeed, the concept of a potential group is questionable. It presumes some a priori group identity. However, group identities develop within the context of group formation. As Arblaster (1993, p. 105) notes:

> 'General interests, like the interests of patients and potential patients, which is what we all are, by their very nature, are not susceptible to organisation or mobilisation in the same way as the interests of specific, permanent groups'.

Perhaps the central problem of pluralism is the tendency to treat business as just another group, but one that is well served in terms of resources. Clearly, business has advantages not available to other groups. First, businesses have ready-made organisations in the form of firms and, consequently, they do not face the collective action problems of other interests (Olson, 1965). Where businesses do have to join together, the benefits of their actions are often enjoyed by a small number of firms and so the incentives to organise are high.

Second, because of its key role in the economy, business has resources unavailable to other groups (Lindblom, 1977). The actions of business affect the lives of many people, and the success of economies as a whole. This, as C. Lindblom points out, gives business a privileged position. Governments need successful economies for their own survival and are therefore inevitably responsive to the interests of business. Third, business has access to financial resources far greater than those of any other group.

Fourth, through ownership of the media, business has much greater access to sources of information than have any other groups. Fifth, business operates within a favourable ideological framework. More or less automatically, business groups are seen as legitimate interests that operate within 'the rules of the game'.

Apparently, in terms of the policy process, pluralist's focus a great deal on the role of groups. In doing so, they underestimate the importance of the state and state actors. Most policies are initiated within the state by state actors. They are not necessarily developing their policy in response to group pressures, but have their own interests which they wish to pursue (Nordlinger, 1981). Frequently, groups are incorporated not because of their pressure but because they are useful to state actors in the development and implementation of policy. It is the state that has the resources and legitimacy to develop and implement policy whilst state actors can, and frequently do, ignore the interests of groups.

Consequently, in examining policy outcomes, the more appropriate focus of analysis may be state organisation rather than group action. An important problem, in terms of British pluralism at least, is that the development of pluralism is culturally and historical specific.) The pluralism of Bentley, Truman and Dahl developed to analyse politics in the USA. In the USA the notion of a strong central state does not exist. At the national level there are competing power centres such as the legislature, judiciary and executive.

In addition, there are important federal and local centres of power. These multiple power centres mean that state actors have an interest in encouraging interest groups into the policy process as a resource for developing and implementing policy, and to provide political support in internal conflicts.

In addition, the weakness of parties, and the failure of

working-class organisations, combined with regional, ethnic and economic divisions means that people often look to interest groups, rather than to parties, to represent their interests. The USA is a political system where interests groups play an important role in the policy process, and the political system is more open to their pressure. It might be the case that a theoretical tradition that developed in the open US system is not applicable to the elitist and closed British state, where ideas of Parliamentary sovereignty and secrecy prevail.

Consequently, it was changing historical conditions that led to a theoretical critique of pluralism. The Vietnam War, the civil rights movement and the persistence of inequality suggested that there were flaws 'in the pluralist heaven'. From the 1960s, pluralism was challenged by a range of alternative theoretical traditions that presented empirical and conceptual criticisms of the pluralist case. Bachrach and Baratz (1962) challenged the notion that power was always exercised through observable behaviour, and proposed that it could be reproduced through keeping issues off the agenda.

Gavanta (1980), among others, questioned Dahl's and Polsby's notion of community power and demonstrated that power within communities, even in the 1960s and 1970s, was still concentrated and cumulative. Mills (1956) and Domhoff (1967) illustrated the range of interconnections between the elites of business, finance, the military and politics that existed in the USA. There might be different elites in various areas of society but these elites were linked through a range of connection, and interchangeable personnel.

Following Mills, Miliband tested the pluralist thesis empirically and found:

> that in terms of social origin, education and class situation, the men who have manned all the command position in the state system have largely, and in many cases overwhelmingly, been drawn from the world of business and property or from the professional middle class.

Remarkably for Miliband, it was not the case that power was dispersed, nor was there a separation between economic and political power.

The theoretical and empirical critique of pluralism was maintained in the 1970s by two very different traditions. First, it was argued that liberal societies were becoming increasingly corporatist. Rather than there being a relatively open process of group/state interaction, groups were developing increasingly integrated relationships with the state. In particular, economic policy decisions were made through a process of bargaining between state actors and the peak economic actors. In Britain, a range of corporatist relationships could be identified in areas such as incomes policy (Crouch, 1977), health policy (Cawson, 1982) and economic policy.

Second, a normative theory of overload was developed. It argued that there were too many groups demanding too much from the government, which was creating overload within the political system. This was making Britain ungovernable. Governments were expected to find solutions to numerous policy problems, and the cost of intervention was bankrupting the state and causing the economy to stagnate. Consequently, rather than pressure groups being good in terms of controlling the state and maintaining the democratic process, they were extending the state too far and undermining democracy by protecting special interests.

The concepts of corporatism and overload inspired the New Right critique of pressure groups. Pressure groups were seen by the New Right as distorting the democratic system. The political process was dominated by groups rather than voters. The result was economic stagnation, as special interests rejected restructuring in order to protect their existing privileges. The dominant political tradition of the 1950s and 1960s was undermined by theoretical inconsistencies, subject to theoretical criticism from Marxists, elitists and the New Right, and challenged empirically because of a range of events in the UK and the USA.

The underlying conception of society was questioned by the political events of the 1960s and 1970s, and the development of corporatism questioned the benign role of pressure groups. The democratic defects of liberal democracy seemed greater than even the most sophisticated pluralists had allowed, and the growth of radical movements that were excluded from the policy process suggested that power was not widely dispersed. However, these problems did not result in the abandonment of pluralism. Rather, a range of pluralist writers attempted to refine their models of power and state-group interaction.

Reformed Pluralism

J.J. Richardson and A.G. Jordan (1979 and Jordan and Richardson, 1987a, 1987b) have recognised that the relationship between the state and pressure groups has changed while maintaining the underlying principles of pluralism. What might be called 'reformed pluralism' accepts many of the criticisms of classical pluralism. It acknowledges that government-interest groups relations are often institutionalised, and that certain groups are excluded from the policy process. Richardson and Jordan (1979, p. 13) admit that '"perfect competition" rarely exists except in theory. In practice we have at best an oligopolist situation and at worst a monopolistic situation'. A group will try to capture a department, which may result in clientelism, with shared priorities and identification between the government agency and the interest group. This has led to the creation of policy communities which blur the distinction between the governed and the governors, and where there is 'cooption and a consensual style' (Richardson and Jordan, 1979, p. 57).

According to Richardson and Jordan, such a model provides for a 'better account for policy outcomes than do examinations of policy stances or of parliamentary influence' (Richardson and Jordan, 1979, p. 74).

However, the key feature of the modern state for reformed pluralists is complexity and fragmentation. The modern polity is segmented. Although there may be closed and institutionalised relationships in one policy or sub-policy area, in other policy areas different groups and interests will be involved, and policy-making may be much more open.

The modern polity is one of conflict between multiple clienteles over the 'collective allocation of scarce resources'. In order to maximise 'legitimacy and autonomy state bureaus create stable networks of clienteles, funding sources and interbureau alliances'.

In spite of these institutionalised arrangements, reformed pluralists do not accept that the state has become a corporate state. For Richardson and Jordan, the notion of a policy community is meant to be a flexible concept.

There is:

> flexibility in the system, not all groups are active in all aspects of even one area as narrowly defined as education.

> On different aspects of policy, different sets of participants are involved. While some groups are very much pare of the department's 'legitimised clientele', others enjoy less comfortable co-existence with the department. Thus it is not possible to give a static and exhaustive listing of groups in a community. (Jordan, 1981, p. 105)

Notably, this conception of flexibility, within structured and institutionalised relationships, leads Jordan *et al.* (1992) to suggest that even areas such as agriculture, which have previously been seen as dominated by very closed relationships with a limited number of groups, are in fact more open than has been presumed:

> The number of interests consulted, the number of interests which civil servants at MAFF acknowledged as influential, and the changed tactics of the NFU in recent years, all tend to support a view of a very dense and specialist policy making terrain (Jordan *et al;* 1992, p. 8).

Reformed pluralism accepts that relationships between groups and the state can be structured and institutionalised. Yet at the same time it tries to retain some of the key features of pluralism. Richardson and Jordan argue that there are no monopolies of power; policy communities include countervailing powers; and the pressure group universe is highly populated.

They believe that these structured relationships are disintegrating and becoming confused, and increasingly open to groups. Reformed pluralism tries to acknowledge the criticisms of pluralism but at the same time retains its key features. Rather than stress the institutionalised forms of state group interaction, they emphasise the ability of groups to break up these relationships. This pluralism is reflected in Richardson and Jordan's view of the consultation process. Although they admit that consultation is often cosmetic, they make continual references to the ease of being consulted, the desire of departments to consult and their long list of consultees.

They also refer to the constraints from Whitehall pluralism and the extent to which there is overlapping membership of policy communities. Hence, their position is very close to that of Truman and Dahl concerning the way overlapping membership of groups prevents a single group from dominating. Richardson and Jordan fail, like classical pluralists, to contextualise the decision-making process. They confuse a large number of groups being involved in decision making with a large number of groups being influential. Groups may be consulted but may exercise little influence, and it is important to understand why some groups have more influence than others.

Back in the USA the response to the criticism of classical pluralism took a number of forms'. As with reformed pluralism, there was an acceptance of what McFarland (1987) calls 'elite pluralism'. Writers such as McConnell (1966) and Lowi (1969) argued that it was increasingly the case that producer groups were coming to dominate particular areas of policy or subgovernments. Within these subgovernments, policy is dominated by an iron triangle of Congressional sub-committee, bureaucratic agency and interest group, who are responsible for the particular policy and who close off the policy area to groups that threaten their interests.

This is a different form of the policy communities outlined by Jordan and Richardson. Nordlinger (1981) attempted an alternative response to the criticism of pluralism. He maintained that policy was not necessarily determined by groups but rather that state actors have their own interests in policy, which they are prepared to defend in the face of group criticism. He therefore acknowledges the role of state officials in determining policy outcomes.

For Nordlinger, pluralism exists within the state as various state officials conflict in order to achieve their particular interests. McFarland (1987), in his sophisticated defence of pluralism, synthesises sub-sectoral government and state autonomy in the 'triadic theory of power'. McFarland distinguishes between iron triangles or 'sub-government power' and 'triadic power'. He accepts that policy areas can be dominated by producer interests. However, the theory of triadic power acknowledges that while economic producer groups will organise in order to lobby the government, in certain situations there will also be countervailing groups that oppose the interests of the producers. At the same time, McFarland appreciates that 'state agencies are normally assumed to have a significant degree of autonomy' (McFarland, 1987, p. 141).

So rather than sub-governments being dominated by iron triangles, within each policy area there is a triad of a state agency with some autonomy, a producer group and countervailing groups. This basic analytic unit is then 'complicated by adding such factors as legislators, presidential policy-makers and the judiciary.

McFarland points out that triads might exist but this does not necessarily mean that all interests are organised. However, it may be the case that countervailing power can limit the strength of producer groups, and this increases the autonomy of agencies. He also argues that in areas of high politics - 'the politics of making general decisions' - presidential policy-makers may greatly restrict the autonomy of agencies.

So, in areas such as deregulation, the intervention of presidential actors can allow a situation where the power of producers is greatly reduced and this increases triadic power. As the reform cycle ends, there may be a shift back to sub-government. McFarland's theory is clearly a useful way of understanding relationships between governments and groups. It is a very sophisticated form of pluralism that recognises the power of producers, the potential of agency autonomy and also the ability of other groups in particular circumstances to restrict the power of producers and the autonomy of the state.

It places policy-making in a context. Its limitations are that, despite its claims, it is not really a theory of power but an analysis of the policy process that is only applicable in particular situations.

Moreover, it bears little relationship to pluralism, being much closer to an elitist analysis of the policy process. An alternative development of pluralism is 'neo-pluralism'.

Neo-pluralism

Further a more radical response to the criticisms of pluralism has been from an approach called neo-pluralism. Neo-pluralism first developed in the USA with the recognition that business was often in a superior position to other groups and enjoys certain advantages over the consumer and the market (Dunleavy and O'Leary, 1987, p. 275). McConnell developed the view that 'the major corporate units of American business exercise great power'. With this power, and the economic needs of war, close relations developed between business and government. Consequently significant parts of government are controlled by business interests (McConnell, 1967, p. 129). For neo-pluralists, countervailing powers are not sufficient to check the interests of business.

Notably, the major development in the theory of neo-pluralism came from an exponent of classical pluralism, Charles Lindblom. For Lindblom, business is advantaged by two important factors. First, government is dependent on a successful economy and so has a tendency to provide inducements and advantages to business. The requirements to meet the needs of business means that it achieves 'a privileged position in government'.

Second, in a market economy, many decisions are taken by business concerning investment and employment. Despite the impact that these decisions have over other people's lives, they are not subject to democratic controls.

These factors led Lindblom to argue that business does not have to operate through the traditional lobbying channels of other pressure groups.

> **Business Benefits from Structural Power:**
>
> Any government official who understands the requirements of his position and the responsibilities that market orientated systems throw on businessmen will therefore grant them a privileged position. He does not have to be bribed, duped or pressured to do so. Nor does he have to be an uncritical admirer of business to do so. He simply understands, as is plain to see, that public affairs in market orientated systems are in the hands of two group leaders, government and business, who must collaborate and that to make the system work government leadership must often defer to business leadership (Lindblom, 1977, p. 175).

The importance of business to the government means that the government will respond automatically to business's interest. Power is structural rather than observable. Lindblom's position is closer to some Marxists than it is 'to pluralists. He acknowledges that power can be exercised in an unobservable way through structures, anticipated reaction and ideology. Yet neo-pluralism still displays some of the features of classical pluralism. It continues to stress the importance of groups and the existence of competitive policy areas. Lindblom distinguishes between grand issues - which are generally closed to the public and concern the major interests of society; and secondary issues - which are not of crucial importance to the state or a key economic interest, and where the policy process is more competitive. Thus neo-pluralism provides a complex and sophisticated view of the modern state. It recognises that business is privileged, but that it does not completely dominate the policy process.

It could be argued that it is a much more realistic analysis of power in the modern state than classical pluralism. Nevertheless, there are a number of problems with neo-pluralism. Neo-pluralism tends to treat business in a very unified and unproblematic manner. It fails to specify the division and conflicts within business and thus the notion of a business veto is oversimplified. Consequently, it does not really specify the nature of structural power and how it operates (Marsh, 1983, p. 7).

Vogel points to the decline of business power since the 1960s and the fact that, with the rise of public interest groups such as consumers and environmentalist, business does not appear to be that successful in vetoing policy (Vogel, 1989). Perhaps what is most important about neo-pluralism is that it represents a convergence between pluralism and Marxism. Changes in modern industrial societies and the collapse of Communism in Eastern Europe nave led' to the questioning- of the traditional theoretical boundaries in political science. To an extent, pluralism has been revitalised by radical political traditions such as post-modernism which are, in part, searching for a theoretical alternative to Marxism.

Postmodernism

It is pertinent to note that of the great ironies of political science is that whilst classical pluralists such as Dahl and Lindblom are shifting towards positions more aligned to Marxism, a number of 'post-Marxists' and post-modernists are rediscovering some of the principal arguments of pluralism.

Again, historical events have influenced the development of pluralism. The crisis of Marxism, resulting from the collapse of Communism, has led a number of Marxists to reconsider the importance of parliamentary democracy and the need to recognise diversity and plurality in civil society (Hindess, 1980). Marxists have also been prepared to accept that the state is not a unified monolith. They see it as conflictual, fragmentary and therefore open to a wider range of interests other than solely business (Jessop, 1990). Consequently, some Marxists have shifted their analysis from privileging class groups and have been prepared to recognise that groups representing other interests can have some influence on policy outcomes.

Indeed, Jessop (1990, pp. 248-9) uses the term 'Marxist pluralists'. The resurgence of pluralism has been taken further by the proponents of post-modernism and radical democracy. Many post-modernists reject what they see as the Marxist belief in a single truth or explanation and its tendency to see inherent characteristics in classes. Frequently, their ideas reflect many of the concerns of pluralism (McLennan, 1989).

As McClure points out: 'this most recent incarnation of pluralism bears certain affinities to its predecessors'.

Indeed, Hirst (1990, p. 47) argues that there is much in classical pluralism that is worth saving. He suggests that pluralism can provide a much more accurate model of how modern liberal democracies operate than can Marxism:

> pluralism provides a theoretical framework which can accommodate both considerable inequality based on socio-economic inequality, and a significant measure of the diffusion of power and influence. It also provides indicators of possible forms of reform that would reduce inequality and would permit the enhanced influence and power of non-wealthy strata. (Hirst, 1990, p. 47)

There are a number of areas where the pluralism of radical democracy and classical pluralism overlap. Both are mistrustful of the state and see voluntary organisations as desirable for controlling the state and as alternative mechanisms for the distribution of public goods.

Consequently, they accept that there can be no organisation that has a monopoly of knowledge. Wainwright (1993) highlights that knowledge is socially constructed; it is impossible for a single person, group or party to know everything; and knowledge can be organised in range of ways. Ideally, knowledge should be demystified and developed in a pluralistic mode through a range of social movements. Thus, central to radical democracy is a strong belief in the richness of civil society and the importance of social movements as a way of controlling and circumventing the monopolising tendencies of the state. Like classical pluralists, radical democrats see social movements as crucial elements in society.

Civil society is complex and pluralistic, with individuals belonging to a vast array of social groups that have no essence but develop as a result of struggle and social interaction (McClure, 1992, p. 115). Wainwright sees the social movements that have developed since the early 1970s as having challenged the traditional position of social democratic movements and as being an important source of social change.

However, unlike the pluralism of the 1950s and 1960s, it is not meant as a realistic portrait of society but as a radical critique of the distribution of power in capitalist societies which offers the alternative of participatory and communitarian politics (Phillips, 1993). In addition, there are significant differences between the epistemologies of radical pluralism and classical pluralism.

Classical pluralism, with its positivist method, maintains the existence of an objective truth. Radical democrats are extreme relativists, arguing that social reality is socially constructed and subject to a range of interpretations, one of which is not inherently more valuable than another. Yet radical democrats make some similar mistakes to classical pluralists. They do not really develop a convincing theory of the state. Radical democrats fail to conceptualise the relationship between the state and civil society and thus are not very effective at developing practical suggestions for overcoming state power.

This leads, like classical pluralism, to an overemphasis on the role of social groups (or social movements). All hope for social change and a radical alternative is vested in social movements which have the potential to bring about radical change. Yet little account is taken of the role of the state in defining and limiting these groups.

Moreover, they are also calling for a radical politicisation of society, where differences can be preserved. But will all social interest be allowed to develop, and who will protect the interest of minorities in a highly politicised and weakly governed society?

To sum up, the main problem in examining pluralism is that no single pluralist theory exists. It is often self-consciously atheoretical and so its assumptions are implicit rather than explicit. This leads to a great deal of confusion among pluralists and their critics about what pluralism is and what it is trying to do. At the same time, pluralism is descriptive, prescriptive and normative. It is also a theory that has been influenced greatly by its historical and social milieux.

It developed within a particular system and has changed significantly according to social and political circumstances. Despite this confusion, pluralism does offer some useful pointers for analysing modern society. Unlike Marxism and elitism, it is aware of the need to understand the complexity of modern society and the implications this has for the state and groups.

Modern liberal democracies are complex and difficult to govern. It is hard to sustain an argument that society as a whole is ruled by a particular class or group. Is any class or group unified enough to rule, and even if it were, does it have the ability to rule information-rich societies that are traversed by a range of social economic cleavages? However, society may be complex and lacking a ruling class, but this does not mean that power is widely dispersed. It is undoubtedly the case, as reformed pluralists point out, that policy-making in liberal democratic society is segmented. In each policy area, different interests prevail.

It is also apparent, as neo-pluralists suggest, that there are certain groups in modern society that have the resources to dominate particular areas of policy making.

There is social closure, and access to the policy process in key areas is heavily restricted. The problem for pluralists is, in a sense, epistemological and methodological. While they are often able to produce empirically useful material, their concentration on the observable means that they are unable to take account of the ideological and the structural as these are not immediately discernible.

It must be remembered that the limits of pluralism lie not in its suggestion that power is a complex phenomena, but in its failure to examine the context in which decisions are made, and the way that such decisions favour some interests over others.

In the next chapter we intend to discuss normative theory of political science in pros and cons.

4

Normative Theory

> "Never make a decision yourself, if you don't have to. When one of your men asks you a question, ask him what is the answer. There is only one answer to many questions, and therefore, this method answers many questions before they are asked. It not only develops your men, but also enables you to measure their ability."
>
> ***—Henry L. Doherty***

Normative political thought finds expression in abstract moral reasoning but also in more detailed discussion of institutions and policies. If in philosophical mode it seeks out - or constructs - guiding moral precepts, in its more concrete applications political theory investigates the implications of moral precepts for actual political practice.

In fact, normative political theory involves, in the words of Isaiah Berlin, 'the discovery, or application, of moral notions in the sphere of political relations'. It is, viewed in these rather narrow terms, a branch of moral philosophy, concerned with the foundational or basic moral questions that affect political life. The remit of the term can, however, be defined more broadly, to cover all political theorising of a prescriptive or recommendatory kind: that is to say, all theory-making concerned with what "ought to be', as opposed to 'what is', in political life.

It is apt to note that normative theory has a long lineage, going back in the West at least to Ancient Greece and in the East to, among other sources, Confucian and Hindu philosophy. Since politics is about 'attending to the general arrangements of a set of people whom chance or choice have brought together' (Oakeshott, 1984, p. 219), normative theorising may appear to be, on the face of it, entirely natural: a way of bringing scholarly attention to the process of 'attending' to our 'arrangements'. Yet the idea of a distinctive field of theoretical activity devoted exclusively to what 'ought to be' has not met with universal acceptance in academic circles. Some critics have denied that human agents exercise meaningful moral choice; others have doubted that moral propositions can be meaningful or derived logically from facts about the world.

In spite of such criticism, normative theory remains a living and vital branch of political studies. Indeed, it has benefited from a considerable revival of interest since the early 1970s, thanks in part to the influence of writers such as John Rawls and Robert Nozick. Its resuscitation follows a long period of retrenchment brought on by the critique from logical positivism in the 1930s and behaviourism subsequently. If for some time now these latter schools have been on the defensive, normative political theorists have displayed increasing confidence. Nonetheless, normative theory faces challenges from new directions.

Salient Features

Normative political theory is a way of talking about social institutions, especially those bound up with the exercise of public power, and about the relationship of individuals to those institutions. It scrutinises the justifications given for existing political arrangements and the justifiability of possible alternative arrangements. Its practitioners employ a variety of methods. Three are typical. Normative theorists are concerned first and foremost with the internal consistency of moral arguments. In measuring this they bring to bear styles of argumentation drawn from, among other sources, formal logic and analytic philosophy. Second, they draw on social science disciplines such as social anthropology and history in order to check the correctness of the empirical premises of arguments, or to expose problems in moral arguments not immediately revealed by abstract reasoning. Finally, normative theorists measure the conclusions of their arguments against their own moral intuitions.

Their arguments may expose the weakness of common-sense intuitions, but equally a conclusion that is strongly counterintuitive may signal a weakness in the reasoning that generated it. Normative theorists will differ in the relative weight they attach to these three elements of abstract logic, social-scientific and historical evidence, and intuition.

The key substantive questions of political theory since the early 1970s can be arranged, very roughly, into two sets. The first centres on the existence and purpose of those public institutions we call the state. Are there moral grounds for a state? If so, for what sort? When should we feel obliged to obey its laws? When, by contrast, is civil disobedience justified?

A second set of substantive questions is concerned with issues of *distributive justice* and its implications for freedom or *liberty*. What is the relative moral importance of freedom and equality? Are there moral grounds for public policies designed to realise some conception of substantive social equality? Would such policies respect the autonomy and liberty of individuals and prove compatible with pluralism?

Political theorists discussing substantive questions are typically drawn to more basic, or *foundational,* issues of moral philosophy. Is there a rationally discernible objective basis to morality? If there is, in what might it consist? Alternatively, is morality a human artefact, the product of convention or community tradition? And why do the answers we give matter for political theory?

Since its 1970s revival, normative theory has developed in a variety of directions. Some of its practitioners have restated the bases of older positions; others (notably the feminists among them) have sought out novel terrain . While not exhausting the field, three broad approaches to normative political theory dominated the debates of the 1970s and subsequently, each drawing on writings of earlier decades and centuries. They are *utilitarianism, deontological liberalism* and *communitarianism.*

1. Utilitarianism

Utilitarianism is a political and moral philosophy associated famously with the radical nineteenth-century social reformer, Jeremy Bentham. Like many subsequent utilitarians, Bentham was suspicious of principles of political action founded on abstract or speculative claims about our natural rights and duties. Bentham appealed instead to what he understood to be basic facts about human nature disclosed by empirical observation. Human beings, he claimed, were motivated by a desire to achieve happiness and to avoid pain. Accordingly, Bentham thought, the *morally* correct political decisions were those which sought the greatest happiness of the greatest number in society. This happiness could be quantified in the form of utility — 'that property in any object whereby it tends to produce benefit, advantage, pleasure, good or happiness' — and the object of policy-makers should be to maximise aggregate social utility.

Notably, Bentham did not seek to prescribe the courses of action which would maximise happiness. The definition of what counts as utility would, in the end, be left to members of society. Each individual should define his or her own good, and in social decision-making the (subjectively defined) interests of each individual should enter equally into the overall 'calculus' of utility. Utilitarianism in this classic form has suffered sustained criticism. The idea that pleasures and pains can be quantified, and that the otherwise incommensurable wants of diverse individuals can be compared impersonally, is widely considered to be implausible.

Many critics have worried about the implications for individual or minority rights of a doctrine that conceives social utility in aggregate terms and refuses the constraints on social action which might be supplied by a theory of rights. Their anxiety is heightened by utilitarianism's reliance on the (expressed) preferences of individuals when some preferences may be highly anti-social (racist, for example).

The injunction to seek the greatest happiness of the greatest number may sanction social engineering or a welfare-orientated technocracy sanctioned by majority consent. Alternatively, its model of the utility-maximising individual could sanction crude free-market apologetics, with the public choice theory of the New Right as its natural successor.

Cultural elitists and religious thinkers fear that the

equating of all wants amounts to a downgrading of the higher things of life, such as good art or divinely ordained truths revealed in the scriptures. One trenchant early critic of Bentham's utilitarianism was John Stuart Mill. Mill eschewed a crudely quantitative utilitarianism in favour of one that accommodated qualitative judgements - allowing, for example, that certain kinds of intellectual or aesthetic experiences might be superior to others equally desired.

Mill also argued for a utilitarianism that protected certain basic or vital interests of all individuals as a matter of right. Rights themselves contribute to general utility by 'making safe the very groundwork of our existence', though whether Mill treats rights as being inviolable in the face of competing imperatives of a utilitarian kind is not completely clear. Mill noted that rights will at times come into conflict with other *rights* and that where they do, only calculations of relative utility can indicate which should prevail.

Mill's arguments mark a departure from 'act-utilitarianism', according to which each act should be judged separately for its happiness-maximising consequences, to 'rule-utilitarianism', which would preserve whole systems of constraining rules because of the benefits they bring to society as a whole (Mill, 1978).

Remarkably, a number of writers since Mill have joined the effort to restate utilitarianism in more acceptable or more persuasive terms. Some have sought a greater subtlety or sophistication for their precepts, others have modified them substantially. While in part the foil of recent debates, utilitarianism has continued to be developed in its own right under a variety of labels - consequenrialism, ideological ethics, proportionalism -and today presents a considerably more elusive target of attack than did its nineteenth century predecessor.

Deontological Liberalism

It is largely in *opposition* to this utilitarian legacy that political theorising revived in the 1970s. Or rather, it took off in opposition to ideological ethics of all kinds. By ideological ethics we mean here moralities that judge the worth of human conduct according to whether it fulfills a particular purpose or realises a particular end or *telos.* Though it does not specify the content of human happiness, utilitarianism is clearly teleological in this sense; but so, for example, is the Aristotelian idea that (male and non-slave) human beings fulfil their rational natures by participating as citizens in the common life of a community.

A number of important thinkers writing in the 1970s - such as John Rawls, Robert Nozick, Ronald Dworkin and Alan Gewirth - insisted that ideological ethics transposed to political life was insufficient or even hazardous for human freedom, for two reasons already alluded to. First, these writers argued, utilitarianism does not take account of the plurality of individual ends - either because it specifies one possible kind of purpose (the maximisation of happiness or utility) as being higher than others, or because it judges human good or welfare from the aggregate vantage point of society as a whole (or of its 'greatest number'), failing to consider each individual separately. Second, teleological ethics gives priority to the ends over the means which might be used to achieve them.

In particular, it refuses to allow that the pursuit of aggregate social goals should be constrained by inviolable *rights* enjoyed by each individual. Whilst, as mentioned above, utilitarians have attempted to address such complaints, their critics maintain that the defence of rights under utilitarianism is always contingent and insecure. Utilitarianism has underpinned much liberal thought, but a number of its critics have declared that liberalism requires a more convincing philosophical grounding.

Notably, writers who made these arguments have come to be known as *deontological* or *Kantian* liberals (Sandel, 1984; Plant, 1993). They contrast deontology (the ethics of right or duty) favourably with teleology (the ethics of ends); and the principal reference point for a deontological ethics is Immanuel Kant. Kant was opposed to any conception of politics that might sacrifice individuals to a higher purpose. Individuals were, for him, ends and not means, and as such they were inviolable.

Kantian liberals believe that individuals should be free to define and pursue their own ends, rather than having the ends of others imposed upon them. If the deontologists have a pluralistic view of human ends, they are not relativists: certain constraints must be placed upon human behaviour, and these should take the form of rights, duties or entitlements that attach to individuals and which cannot be overridden. Individuals are free and autonomous beings, but they should not be free to violate the freedom and autonomy of others.

They may pursue separate 'goods', but they must proceed within a framework of commonly agreed or universally respected 'rights'; and where the right and the good conflict, right should prevail. Liberals insist that *collective* social action too must respect individual rights, which all deontological liberals insist includes a strong right to liberty. At the same time, liberals are distinguished from anarchists by acceptance that a public body of some kind is needed to guarantee rights and to make them effective.

Even determinedly free market liberals recognise that in order to fulfill its most essential functions, the public body in question - the stare - must subject individuals to laws that regulate their behaviour or make demands on their private resources (for example, through taxation). The role of the state becomes more controversial among deontological liberals who suggest that it seeks to satisfy welfare as well as libertarian rights. At this point a whole host of problems arise.

What precisely is the state required, or entitled, to do? Should it simply maintain law and order, or intervene to redistribute wealth? Is there such a thing as a right to a certain minimum of welfare? If individual rights against the state are inviolable, what exactly are those rights? Those arguing for universal human rights court more than just academic controversy. They are speaking to a world marked by the decline of universalistic projects such as socialism and liberalism; growing national, religious and territorial fragmentation; and by the advance of an identity politics amongst women and ethnic minorities.

In such a world the ground for cross-cultural agreement about universal rights often seems tenuous. Of course, defenders of universal rights will insist that the current multiplication of inter-community conflicts only underlines the need to find some universally agreed yardsticks for adjudicating contending ethnic and cultural claims. That, indeed, is my own view.

But there are important currents of normative theory whose exponents doubt that such a universal vantage point is either possible or desirable. Some feminists argue that the supposedly universal vantage point of liberal normative theory is in fact a male one: impersonal, abstract, rational and public, in contrast to the empathetic, practical and localised way in which women more comfortably address human disputes (Brown, 1993). Here I shall focus on another approach critical of deontology, that loosely referred to as *communitarian*.

2. Communitarianism

Communitarians begin with a critique of the liberal concept of the individual self. The liberal self is, as Michael Sandel puts it, 'unencumbered' - able to adopt a vantage point outside the community of which it is part, and to define and redefine its aims and commitments without reference to inherited traditions or shared goals. It is endowed with rights and duties specified in purely abstract and universal terms that discount the claims and obligations arising from our own personal and social ties. Communitarians believe that the individuated self of liberalism is dominant only where communal ties have become eroded and individuals find themselves alienated and adrift, though even here communal life or tradition is the necessary reference point of individual dissent.

Normatively they consider such individualism undesirable, a symptom of something wrong. They prefer to speak of a 'situated' self -one that is embedded in a community and defined by the attachments and shared self-understandings which frame community life. It is from our community - whether it is a village or sub-culture or movement or ethnic group - that we derive the specific rights and obligations that make up our 'moral particularity'. At the same time we are necessarily 'implicated in the purposes and ends' of our community.

A conception of rights and duties as particular to communities, and of purposes as shared by them, conflicts sharply with the deontological liberal commitment to universal rights and individually particular ends. Communitarians are suspicious of the way deontologists insist that right (universal principles of justice) must constrain, or set boundaries on, pursuit of the collective good.

The deontological liberals argue that since we cannot fully understand other people's ends, any societal pursuit of a higher social end will impose itself on the self-understandings of individuals who make up society. Sandel, on the other hand, insists that the shared life of a community can reduce this mutual opacity, allowing certain common self-understandings to emerge among people and, with these, goals which are genuinely common and not imposed. In Sandel's eyes, liberals devalue the good by leaving its definition open to the calculations of self-interested individuals. In a community, by contrast, there exists the prospect that all might work towards a morally worthy common good.

Notably, if communitarians are suspicious of rights-based liberalism, they do not unite behind any common political alternative. Writers from a wide variety of ideological backgrounds have sought recourse in communitarian positions. They include the conservative writer Michael Oakeshott, attracted by communitarianism's defence of particularity ana tradition against universalistic rationalism; and civic republicans such as Hannah Arendt and Michael Sandel, drawn to the prospect of a participatory public life.

Today they attract a new strand of political thinkers wishing to recreate a sense of communal obligation between people on the ashes of what they perceive as the tailed individualism of both the New Right and the New Left (see, for example, Etzioni, 1993). If communitarianism proceeds from a critique of liberalism, it is itself vulnerable to the objection that it offers insufficient safeguards to individual liberty or protection against traditionalist or majoritarian tyranny.

Some strands of communitarian thought connect with conservative notions of organic community in which moral conformity is stressed at the cost of individual dissent. Other strands allow for the possibility of a participatory or democratic community but, liberty defenders might argue, leave the individual vulnerable to a heteronomous majoritarian will. The vision of democracy by consensus which some radical communitarians advance as an alternative to majoritarianism is arguably impractical in a world of culturally individuated people, or one in which scarcity and conflicts of interest are ineradicable.

The attempt to operate the rules of 'unitary democracy' in a diverse community moreover threatens to marginalise the (often distinctive) interests of those who are less effective participators (Mansbridge, 1980). The more liberty-sympathetic or democratic-minded communitarians might reply that they envisage participation in, or identification with, only *some* kinds of community, and that widespread individual dissociation from common life is a symptom of the fact that a community no longer exists.

The question for such communitarians is not whether individual dissent should be suppressed—it should not be—but how a community might be created that all can feel (undissentingly) a part of. Given that cohesive communities have become increasingly rare, and that they are difficult to recreate in today's mobile, globally interdependent world, this reply arguably leaves communitarianism in a condition of either pessimism or impotent utopianism. More important, seen from a liberty-protective standpoint, such an argument offers no good reason for downgrading individual rights. The guarantee of those rights could be considered necessary not only in the long period which must precede the successful recreation of communal life but, if experience of authoritarianism in some past communal experiments is anything to go by in any kind of commune we can hope realistically to create in the future. Nevertheless, communitarianism does offer some powerful arguments. It makes us conscious of the way our inherited tradition shapes the way we reason morally, so that even in opposition to it we may find ourselves having to engage its language

It reminds us that we are born with moral obligations as a community that we can only disown by sounding insensitive to those to whom our predecessors incurred moral debts (think here of Germans born after 1945 and the special responsibility ley might have in fighting Fascism or racism). Communitarianism shows us further how some moral obligations we incur are to the people immediately around us, be they our family, friends or community, and that abstract moral language works better in public life than in the more informal and mutually empathetic life of, say, a group of acquaintances. In the tatter's company it may often be more appropriate to act out of love or personal loyalty, in a spirit of protective paternalism or in ways that draw in intimate knowledge, rather than according to the impersonal and undifferentiating principles favoured by deontologists.

Finally, the communitarian ideal of social solidarity addresses a genuine deficiency of our atomised modern life and is probably shared by many who defend individual rights.

A Critical Analysis

The range of positions recovered or generated in the

political theorising since the 1970s is, it is clear, very wide. The disagreements internal to political theory between utilitarians, deontologists, communitarians and others (as well as within these camps) sometimes run very deep. However, it may also be helpful to consider the views of some of those who doubt that the enterprise of normative theory is possible at all.

Logical Positivism

Logical positivism is a school of analytic philosophy inspired in pan by the early writings of Ludwig Wittgenstein, in particular his *Tractatus Logico-Philosophicus* (1921). The *Tractatus* is a study of the logic of language: of what makes it meaningful or gives it the capacity to communicate truth. The elemental units of language which give it that power are, he concludes, names: for only names refer directly to the world outside language. Their meaning is not mediated by other propositions of language: they have external objects *as* their meaning.

Conversely, only propositions which refer to external objects can be true. The sole exceptions here are tautological propositions, which are always true by definition, and contradictory propositions, which are always false, again by definition. Wittgenstein did not himself specify the nature of the objects to which true propositions refer, but other logical positivists have insisted that they should be material objects or direct sense experiences.

If that is so then normative theory is, as R. Plant puts it, 'in deep trouble', for its component parts - words like liberty and justice - do not refer to objects of a material or sensually-experienced kind. Wittgenstein himself considered the propositions of ethics, aesthetics, religion and metaphysics to be 'nonsense', and held that philosophy should confine itself to the factual or descriptive language of natural science.

This pretty much set the tone for subsequent condemnations of 'metaphysics' by the two schools of political studies which logical positivism certified as capable of telling objective truths about the world: behaviourial political science and the linguistic analysis of political concepts. Both behaviourists and linguistic analysts insisted on separating factually or logically true propositions from 'values', which in their view issued from emotions, sentiments and attitudes.

Their writings suggested that normative theory was about subjective values and could never aspire to the status of a hard intellectual or scientific discipline. How have normative theorists responded to such charges? One response has been to concede that moral propositions are not facts or logically derivable from facts, but to insist that this does no serious damage to the prospects of a rigorous normative theory.

In the first place, normative theory can make *use* of 'facts' or, at any rate, of the evidence and arguments which come from the descriptive disciplines of social science. The nature of reality 'as it is' - in so far as we can know or understand it -is not immaterial to normative theorists. It has been cited in arguments about, for example, the universality or particularity of human traits and needs. While it cannot derive values from facts, normative theory can disclose the logical relationships implicit in a particular moral discourse. Since the members of a moral community rarely subject their everyday language to rigorous examination, normative theorists do perform a special kind of service here, often to exacting standards.

Further, a more ambitious response from normative theory insists that moral truths *can* be shown to have objective foundations. Alan Gewirth argues that rights to freedom and well-being can be deduced by strict logic from certain basic or generic requirements of human action (Gewirth, 1978). John Rawls seeks a moral argument which if not 'factual' is nevertheless not a product of particular values either. Rawls believes he can find this in the procedural device of the 'original position', where he tries to imagine the principles of justice that would be chosen by founders of a new order who have no prior knowledge of their natural endowments, social resources, status and so on - people who are forced to devise principles neutral enough to cover *any* prospective member of the future society, since *they* could be any one of those members.

Even if Gewirth can demonstrate a strict logical link between a human right to freedom and well-being and certain facts about the requirements of human action, it is not clear what that would prove, since a person not sharing Gewirth's methodology could deny that rational consistency carries moral salience, or that the rational consistency of a moral proposition with a fact makes it a fact. Similarly, Rawls' brilliant idea of the original position is best seen, as Ronald Dworkin would have it, as a device whose choice in the first place reflects an antecedent moral commitment to equal concern and respect for human beings (Dworkin, 1977).

Factual argumentation is salient to normative theory, but normative theory is not a variant of it.

Relativism

Moral relativists, the second group of critics I wish to consider, might argue that if morals cannot be derived from facts then they are indeed, in the final instance, purely relative. And if they are purely relative — if no one value position can be described as better than another — then there is no point in normative theory as such.

If moral claims are fiercely contested, yet at the same time matters of opinion rather than fact, how might one ever adjudicate them? Communitarians answer that particular moralities may still have a role where transcendent ones are forgone: certain things may still be morally right *within* a particular community and its language game, even where they are hot universally right or wrong.

Pure moral relativism would require that every individual be an island: but the nature of language is that we are not, and that moral and other meanings are intersubjectively constituted. *Ipso facto,* there is still a place for morality in the world, and indeed for normative theorists who set out to explicate in a coherent and deep way what it is that a community's own cultural language entails in moral terms. This answer will not quite do. Moral argument in today's world does not take place in hermetically sealed language games.

Language games encounter each other when countries go to war, when they give each other economic or military aid, when they trade or pay debts, when they join common organisations and subscribe to common charters. If there is not as such a coherent global moral community, it is none the less clear that moral languages overlap, cross-cut, mix, engage with each other and shift in response to external pressures. A communitarian might argue that if such fluid interaction heightens the possibility of a collision of moral language games, it requires all the more urgently that each be accorded equal respect, the better to avoid conflict or imposition.

But this kind of reasoning seems plausible only up to a point. In some situations it may legitimate oppression within moral communities or abolish all agreed criteria of conflict resolution between them, thus confounding the aims of a communitarian pluralism. The pure celebration of moral and cultural differences will not help if another community's language game allows that your own territory be seized, or that one of your citizens be sentenced to death by a foreign power, or that their pollution should rain down on your forests and fields.

There is at least a case, one might argue, for seeking cross-communal clarity about the criteria that might reasonably be used to adjudicate the competing claims of moral communities sharing spaces or resources. What, in any case, *is* a moral community? It is difficult to see, say, a nation state as one, when most entities the size of a nation state will be certain to harbour differences of moral perception.

Groups or individual dissidents in one nation state may feel oppressed by their own rulers and appeal to other nation states for help. Individuals may form group allegiances that cut across national boundaries. Again it is difficult to see an ethnic group or a sex as a moral community in the bounded sense. Perhaps only a genuinely voluntary association of consenting adults can be that. Bur even *it* participates in a wider moral universe when it interacts with others outside that association.

Remarkably, the strongest reply from normative theory to moral relativism is that there are certain basic precepts recognised as being morally right by at least some people across virtually all boundaries of moral community. The wrongness of torture is not a 'fact', but recognition of it has a beach-head wherever someone is being tortured, unless that person genuinely consents to being tortured. In other words, there are community-transcending moral language games that are also, in this sense, universal ones.

The claim here is not that any given precept can be shown to have been present in all societies at all times, nor that all widely accepted precepts are just. It is simply that the cultural relativity of moral language does not itself serve as a plausible defence of an outrage in a world where we all speak to each other about morals, still less where we all claim to have signed up to some common moral rules. If moral discourse cuts across cultural boundaries the argument against universalising moral theory from the standpoint of multiple language games loses much of its force.

Determinism

Further, a final argument against normative theory comes from determinism. There are bodies of theory which appear, at least on a certain reading, to deny that human beings exercise the powers of agency that are a precondition of moral choosing. There is no sense in judging a course of action to be morally blameworthy if those who carried it out had no real choice but to do so.

Someone who is forced at gunpoint to kill another is generally not considered to be as culpable as someone who carefully plans and premediates a murder. Are there senses in which all of us are deprived of morally relevant choices, or in which our choices are at any rate more limited than normative theory supposes?

It is remarkable that many types of determinism can be distinguished. Some might regard the individual agent as determined, or at least very strongly constrained and pressured, by external forces beyond his or her control.

Individuals might be subject to hidden structures or to unfolding historical processes driven by internal and impersonal logic. Forces or relationships associated with economic life are commonly attributed a more or less determining role in currents of both Marxism and liberalism; other determinists might stress national traditions or ecological constraints; and still others, supernatural forces. A second kind of determinism might hold that we are determined by forces inside ourselves beyond our control, such as our subconscious, or our genetic inheritance.

It might even be said that there is no consciousness outside of brain processes, and so therefore no moral command centre not itself reducible to the firing of distinctive coalitions of pre-wired neurons. So in what sense are we free to make moral choices? Is there, indeed, a 'we' to do the choosing? There are many components to the determinist case, and not all can be addressed here. I shall consider just two of the questions it raises. The first is whether the advocate of a determinist position is himself or herself amoral. A Marxist of determinist bent may still consider capitalism to be unjust and socialism just (Geras, 1985).

A Freudian convinced of the power of the subconscious may still consider it desirable that a patient be shown the way to greater mental health. In these senses they may still make normative judgements; they may, indeed, have begun their research in order to solve a moral or normative 'problem', such as the existence of capitalism or neurosis. Moreover, value positions often lurk behind - or seek justification in - ostensibly value-free claims about ineluctable causal connections between phenomena such as, to cite one example, human nature and greed. Of course the presence of value assumptions in a scholarly enterprise does not show that its conclusions are false - but we should be alert to those values none the less, since they give us a deeper understanding of the strengths, weaknesses and larger significance of an intellectual project. The second question is whether moral reasoning, as an intellectual activity, is judged to have a role in determining historical or personal outcomes. This is the really important question for the prospects of normative theory. There may be forces that constrain us, but do they leave us with important choices?

In the making of those choices, can we be influenced by arguments about the rightness or wrongness of courses of action? Alternatively, can those who shape the behavioural sanctions and incentives that regulate us be so influenced? If the answers to these questions are 'yes', then normative theory has a 'role'. Two things can be said here for normative theory, both of a tentative kind. The first is that it would be very difficult to demonstrate that we are *never* left with important and morally salient forms of choosing: even the previously mentioned person at gunpoint has *some* choice (between killing and being killed) and there are many situations in life where the range of choice available to us is much larger than in that scenario.

Many writing in supposedly determinist currents (like Marxism) would readily concede a place to human agency within variously understood contexts of structural constraint. If we *do* exercise meaningful choice, it seems at least plausible that moral language can influence the choices we make. Moral discourse is a part of our cultural environment, a part of the way cultures are communicated and reproduced. Of course we encounter moral language in many forms, and that part of it presented to us in theoretically explicit ways is just one of them. None the less, rigorous moral talk may count for something, especially among certain kinds of opinion-forming elites, such as educators, legal theorists and political thinkers.

It will be most influential in legalistic cultures or cultures which esteem scholarship. Where participants in moral conversation are self-doubting, uncertain about an issue, or on a particular matter are disinterested, moral theory may help clarify their views, give expression to their inarticulate feelings or persuade them to modify views inconsistent with other things they believe. This section has defended normative theory against the claims of positivism, relativism and determinism. The case for normative theory implicit in it may now be summarised more positively.

Normative theory offers a medium for giving logically rigorous and factually informed consideration to human moral options in those areas where human beings have moral options - that is to say, where they exercise something we can recognise as free moral agency. Areas of moral choice may sometimes be considerable, and within their boundaries moral theory can make a difference.

There is, of course, no guarantee that the difference it makes will be for the better, or that the approaches generated by normative theory will be 'good' ones (they will in any case be many). Engagement with normative theory nevertheless proceeds from the hope that moral actors who debate their options in an open and self-conscious way will, on the whole, do fewer of the things most of us would consider bad than those who proceed unreflectively or suppress moral debate.

Applied Normative Theory

It is pertinent to note that one important area of

application of normative theory is justice, or the distribution of goods. Here normative theorists have reached into the heart of — and arguably have influenced - one of the most persistent and hard-fought controversies in post-1930s Western political life: how far should the state intervene to structure or pattern, the distribution of goods in society? It is a debate which has raged against the background of the growth, (and, since the mid-1970s, the economic and legitimation crises) of the 'welfare state'.

Remarkably, one camp in this debate may be called, very roughly, *social democratic:* the camp which argues or implies that there are moral grounds for the state to engage in forms of social provision or redistribution of goods. Since such actions involve coercive transfers of resources from some citizens to others, how might they be justified in societies that claim to respect individual autonomy and liberty? Several answers are possible. A defence of the welfare state might be made on the utilitarian ground that it ensures the greatest happiness for the greatest number; for example, because those who have few goods gain a greater utility from obtaining at least some, or because welfare economics raises general welfare by boosting aggregate demand.

The deontological objection to such arguments is that they subordinate individual rights to a single concept of welfare. At the same time they leave welfare itself on an insecure footing. So what strategies are open to social-democratic deontological liberals? The strategy made famous by John Rawls is that of the 'original position'. Rawls asks us to imagine the founders of a state who have no advance knowledge of their talents or prospects or social ranking in the new order. From behind this 'veil of ignorance' they must select the principles of justice that will govern the distribution of primary social goods such as well-being and liberty.

Rawls believes they will choose two principles: a First Principle of equal liberty, which enjoys special priority, and a Second Principle, which permits only those inequalities in the distribution of goods that benefit the least advantaged. Though inviolable, the principles chosen allow for a plurality of ends in the distribution of all but primary goods. Moreover, they are in theory compatible with a wide variety of socioeconomic systems, from capitalism to democratic socialism.

A second deontological strategy finds warrant for intervention in the market in a foundational principle that is categorical and needs no justification. This is the approach of Ronald Dworkin, for whom the basic principle in question is equal concern and respect for human beings (Dworkin, 1977).

Dworkin asks what it means for a government to treat its citizens equally. He notes (using American nomenclature here) that conservatives and liberals will come up with different answers. He then sets out to explicate the liberal answer. He believes such a government will take equally seriously the different ends and preferences of its citizens. It cannot do this by distributing goods centrally according to uniform criteria, and so must allow the workings of a market.

However, it is not only preferences that are differentiated: so are people's talents, levels of inherited wealth and special needs. In a free market these will translate into inequalities of outcome which liberals cannot defend. The liberal will therefore seek to reform the market, and will probably turn to a mixed economic regime - 'either redistributive capitalism or limited socialism' (Dworkin, 1984, p. 69). A third possible justification of state provision would follow from a theory of basic and universal human needs. The problem here, of course, is that there is little agreement (say, across cultures) about what constitute the 'primary goods' of human beings. Whatever the diversity of ends that humans might choose, certain basic requirements must be met — the generic requirements of voluntary and purposive action — before they can even begin to act as moral agents. These requirements include both freedom and well-being. To these there is a universal right. The right to well-being cannot, however, be satisfied limitlessly without contravening the right to freedom. As with Dworkin, Gewirth comes out in favour of a meliorative 'supportive state' rather than either the free market or full substantive egalitarianism (Gewirth, 1978). A fourth approach is communitarian. Michael Walzer, in his *Spheres of Justice,* argues that proper distributive criteria vary not only between cultures and communities but also between different 'spheres of justice' such as security and welfare, money and commodities, office, hard work, free time, education, love and divine grace.

He argues for a 'complex equality' designed to ensure that the distributive criteria salient to one sphere do not impinge on other spheres where different criteria are appropriate. In a market society this may mean giving special attention to preventing those who legitimately have a certain amount of money from using it to, say, buy people, or office, or honour, or exemption from military service: commodities money should not be permitted to buy.

In the sphere of security and welfare there must be a more or less extensive system of communal provision in recognition of need and membership of a community: but since definitions of need and basic goods vary, there can be no universal individual *right* to any particular set of goods beyond the right to life and basic subsistence. Beyond these the appropriate policies of redistribution will flow from shared community understanding and shifting political determination (Walzer, 1985). All these positions allow that redistributions can be morally legitimate. It is this conclusion which *libertarians* regard as an infringement of basic liberties and as supplying ultimately a licence for totalitarianism.

Libertarians may be of Left or Right, but it is those of the Right - the free marketeers - that have mounted the more influential challenge to social democratic or welfarist ideas. Free market libertarians range in turn from outright anarchists who refuse any kind of state authority.

Why do libertarians consider such interventions a threat to basic rights and freedoms? It is helpful here to introduce a basic distinction, famously discussed by Isaiah Berlin, between 'negative' freedom, defined in terms of the absence of coercive constraints on action; and 'positive' freedom, defined as the power to achieve desired ends or to achieve self-mastery.

Berlin (1984) believes that only the former is properly counted as freedom. Policies to enable individuals to achieve their ends may be justifiable, even where they involve coercion of others - this would be so in the case of helping the poor via taxation - but they should not be considered as increasing freedom.

Free market libertarians concur in a definition of liberty purely in negative terms. They are extremely reluctant to see any part of this liberty traded off for some other social good. Coercive state social intervention by definition abridges individual negative liberty. Such abridgement is, according to libertarians, both morally unjustifiable and deleterious to social welfare. This is the argument of, for example, F. A. von Hayek. Hayek believes that the only possible basis of social freedom and economic success is the self-directing individual. Individuals should have equal access to negative liberty, secured through the rule of impersonal laws and regulations that allow them to pursue their own ends within the law. State distribution of income or wealth violates not only liberty but also equality. It requires that the state determine rules of distribution which discriminate against some individuals and in favour of others.

These rules cannot be devised on uncontroversial criteria and are inevitably arbitrary in their effects. Nor can state distribution be justified as a corrective to social injustice. To argue that a given distribution of goods is unjust is to imply that it constitutes a deliberately intended outcome for which redress might be sought. Injustice can only result from the malign intentions of particular individuals. In a free market society, distributions are the result of the unintended consequences of countless voluntary transactions.

There is thus no party from which redress might legitimately be exacted. Hayek also argues that state economic and social intervention produces failure. He dislikes the assumption that complex human societies can be planned rationally, arguing that this fails to register the limits of human knowledge. Spontaneously-evolved institutions resulting from the unintended effects of voluntary transactions among large numbers of people are, he argues, more likely to be successful than institutions deliberately designed by a supposedly omniscient centre.

Robert Nozick develops his own distinctive libertarian position. He disagrees with anarchist arguments against a state, favouring instead a minimal state that restricts itself to maintaining law and order. He rejects all other kinds of intervention on the grounds that they violate individual autonomy as conceived by Kant: instead of treating individuals as ends in themselves, they use some individuals without their consent for some supposedly higher purpose, such as the achievement of a particular distribution of goods. Nozick develops a particular theory of property ownership that he terms 'historical'.

He argues that if a person's holdings came to him or her by a just process of aquisition or transfer, no government could justly transfer a part of those holdings to another without consent. The pursuit of a 'patterned' distribution of goods at a particular time violates historically-inherited entitlements to property. This, of course, raises the question of how just entitlements to holdings are acquired in the first place. Here Nozick uses a Lockean argument: we acquire entitlements by mixing our own labour — which we own — with unowned resources. Provided this primary aquisition does not worsen the situation of others at that time, it is just. All inequalities resulting from the subsequent use and free exchange of holdings is just so long as the initial appropriation of resources is just.

Notably, there is no space here to debate the merits of these various libertarian and social democratic arguments. A brief concluding comment can, however, be made. None of the above arguments is uncontested. Each raises a host of problems. In my view those posed by the libertarian arguments are more acute. It can be argued that Hayek overstates the extent to which given distributions of goods constitute an unforeseen outcome; it may be that inegalitarian outcomes are the predictable result of a certain kind of exchange system, and that the participants in its exchanges are aware of these external consequences of their private transactions.

Arguably, Nozick cannot demonstrate why 'labour mixing' should carry the moral weight that it does, nor why all voluntary exchanges of justly acquired property are just, even where, say, those exchanges are structurally unequal. The argument that free markets bring the greater benefits to the poor carries moral weight, but of a utilitarian kind, and still awaits historical verification. Arguments about the right to goods may be problematic in their own ways, the social democratic (and leftwards) camp shows that there are strong moral arguments for redistribution. Those who accept a Dworkian premise - that human beings deserve to be treated with equal concern and respect - cannot treat as morally neutral the inegalitarian results of economic systems (such as the market) that are products of history and convention rather than of natural or purely spontaneous human activity.

And writers such as Gewirth do demonstrate something incontrovertible: that to be a freely choosing agent we must have both liberty and well-being. More than that can be said: to be active participants in politics, and thus collectively self-determining, we may need access to politically relevant resources on a roughly equal basis. Substantive (if rough) equality may be a precondition of equal political agency.

An Assessment

The big issues facing normative theory can be 'summarised' in many ways. One is whether normative theory is possible at all. I have laid out a few of the arguments *against*—positivists, revisit and determinist—and suggested that none finally establishes its case contrary to the claims of its critics, normative theory can offer vigorous and informed way of addressing options open to human beings whose spares of life in which they can exercise free moral agency. The second major question is internal to relative theory. Which decisions about human goods should be left to individuals privately, or political communities collectively, to determine according to their preferences, and which should be either contained or guided by fundamental principles?

It is unhelpful to divide participants in normal political debates into revisits on the one hand and those claiming to be identified objective moral principles on the other.

The utilitarians deontologists and communitarians all seek their fixed points, and it would leave certain important matters to individuals, democratic or community decisions. The classic utilitarians find their point of fixed the assumption of a rational, utility-maximising individual, in the scientific hope that it might be possible empirically to measure and compare references, and in the principle of utility itself.

On the question of the rural content of utility they are, however, relativists of a sort. The utilitarians at least are relativist also in so far that they would not council the individual's free choice of ends by unassailable natural right claim. The deontologists find their fixed point in a variety of starting points method, human nature or social contracts—and in the principle of fundamental, trans-historical claims of right and justice.

On the other hand, there content to leave the choice of ends to individuals themselves, viewing principles of right and justice in part as the necessary groundwork for the free choosing. Finally, communitarians tie moral obligation to community, eschewing the individualistic relativism of the other two camps the same time they allow for an inter-community relativism, denied the universal moral vantage point of the 'unencumbered self'. In my own view, these three camps all off important arguments. Benthamite utilitarianism itself largely to hourious. However, the idea that the moral worth of human conduct to be established without any reference to the benefits and harms it bring seems perverse, and it is doubtful that even a hardened deontologist would wish to claim that it can be.

The morally relevant harms and benefits in ration may be those that follow from observing certain rules rather than individual actions; they may accrue to individuals over some longer than or in ways that are difficult to specify in narrowly practical terms monologists, who argue for the recognition of rights, or for something prior to rights, such as equal concern and respect for human beings, must have in mind the thought that violating these rights and precepts will bring harm.

If observing them brought nothing but centuries of historically-proven misery, even deontologists would think twice about advocating them. Nevertheless, the deontological tradition itself generates arguments which no utilitarian, consequentialist or proportionalist can ignore comfortably. It is all very well to talk of harms and benefits, but can these simply be weighed up so that wherever aggregate totals of benefit outweigh harms, a course of action can be considered proper?

Again, it is intuitively sensible to take account of consequences, but what kinds of consequence count as acceptable? If a policy brings benefit to many but intolerable harm to a few, is it therefore to be judged as being morally acceptable? Here, only a hardened utilitarian could say that it can be. Deontology stipulates criteria which any just outcome must satisfy. It appeals to the conviction that individuals cannot be treated unfairly, or as means to ends, or be deprived of liberty and well-being. The weighing of harms and benefits of public policies will not, even where each agent's preference counts for one, automatically respect this conviction.

Paradoxically, deontology might disclose where ruder calculations of cost and benefit become acceptable: where fundamental rights are not at stake, perhaps, or where they conflict. Because it often makes 'foundationalist' assumptions about human nature or need, deontology will also be more open to the possibility that some rights exist which are not disclosed by our immediate subjective preferences, and that their protection is a precondition to pursuing our individually or democratically chosen ends. The main problem with communitarianism is that it is reluctant to accept that individual rights might be appealed to against community morality, or to recognise that community moralities meet each other in a globalised moral village.

Though endorsing a pluralism *of* moral communities, it lacks a principle of individual rights in which to anchor a normative commitment to pluralism *within* (all) moral communities. Of the three traditions, however, communitarianism is the only one to remind us that important areas of decision-making are not of the public kind to which abstract rules can easily be applied; and that in public life itself, collective democratic decision-making and participation themselves properly decide a lot of what we are entitled, or obliged, to do.

The preceding discussion makes obvious the different aspects of normative theory.

In the next chapter we will deal with the rather new theory of Marxism as a political thought.

5

Marxist Theory: An Evaluation

> "Work is all important because that is the only visible and intelligible excuse for our existence. Man expresses the forces with which he is endowed. Work is the most satisfying experience of the day."
>
> —*David Sarnoff*

As G. Lukacs observed, it had become an increasingly precarious task to challenge or reject particular theses without forfeiting the right to the title 'Marxist'. Such a thankless task has not become any easier with the passage of time. In part, this can be attributed to the problems experienced within the Marxist tradition during the 1970s. The doubts which had surrounded structuralist Marxism had developed into a full-blown crisis as the pivotal role accorded to class struggle was questioned increasingly. This was a problem accentuated by the emergence of new issues such as feminism and environmentalism, the persistence (some would say success) of the welfare state, and the transformation of work relations under capitalism.

Although not always directly concerned with the debates on state theory, these issues have nevertheless had a profound impact on its development (for a more detailed account of these themes, see Taylor (1994)). It is also important to recognise that Marxist state theory has also had a profound effect on other traditions, and has influenced the work of notable political scientists such as Andrew Gamble and Charles Lindblom.

Marx on the State

It is possible to discern in Marx's writings at least two analytically distinct accounts of the relationship between the state and particular classes. The first, and by far the most influential, is the view of the state as an instrument of the dominant class which performs the crucial function of co-ordinating its long-term interests. From this perspective, most commonly associated with the Communist manifesto, Marx argues that the 'executive of the modern State is but a committee for managing the affairs of the whole bourgeoisie' (Marx, 1973, p. 69).

Here, Marx depicts class struggle in terms of a simple clash between two opposites, with a declining number of the bourgeoisie and an explosion in the size of the proletariat. The second view embodies a more subtle appreciation of the relationship between the state and particular classes. Such a view can be seen clearly in Marx's essays on contemporary political events in France, *18th Brumaire of Louis Bonaparte* (1852) and *Class Struggles in France* (1850), where he is eager to stress the plurality of classes and the manner in which the state appears capable both of dominating civil society and of restricting the power of the bourgeoisie.

While this analysis suggests that agents of the state do not simply perform the function of co-ordinating the long-term interests of the dominant class, Marx was nevertheless convinced that the state's role could not escape indefinitely the constraints imposed by those who own and control the means of production. There arc, then in Marx's work, two distinct approaches to the relationship between the state and particular classes. On one hand, the state is viewed, as being relatively autonomous from the dominant class, and on the other, it is depicted as an instrument serving the interests of the dominant class. It should be noted, however, that these early essays do not establish a coherent and reasoned analysis of the state.

As Jessop notes, at best they can be considered as a set of arguments which display an interest in the relationship between the state and class struggle within a general framework of historical materialism (Jessop, 1982, p. 9). Marx's failure to elucidate this relationship in a more systematic manner meant that the task fell to the next generation of Marxists, most notably Georgi Plekhanov and Karl Kautsky.

However, stimulated by the desire to establish a scientific Marxism (dialectical materialism) capable of replacing bourgeois science, these authors emphasised the determining role of the productive forces at the expense of the relations of production (economism). Economism is a variant of Marxism which overemphasises the determination of social life by the economic base and therefore underestimates the importance of ideology and political action in the formation of history.

It also embraces the view that there exist a set of objective laws of historical development. Put simply, this second generation of Marxists produced an evolutionary-determinist conception of history in which capitalism was governed by a set of immutable laws that lay beyond the scope of man (economism) (Merrington, 1978).

As a consequence, Marxism had been cleansed of its humanist and philosophical bias and was now firmly rooted in a scientific prescription of the inevitable collapse of capitalism. This position, undoubtedly influenced by the publication of Charles Darwin's *Origin of Species,* was well suited to the political practice of the second international workers' movement. More importantly, for the purposes of this chapter, it was the rejection of this political and theoretical orthodoxy that formed the starting point of Antonio Gramsci's attempt to reformulate the Marxist theory of the state.

Antonio Gramsci

The power and originality of Gramsci's arguments lie undeniably in his attempt to re-establish human subjectivity as the principal feature of Marxism. In the orthodox Marxism of Kautsky and Plekhanov priority lay with the objective conditions of capitalism; human subjectivity (consciousness) was therefore seen as the simple manifestation of a series of deeper economic processes.

In contrast, all of Gramsci's most significant contributions to Marxist theory represent an attempt to restore the voluntarist side of Marxist theory: a concern with the role of ideas, consciousness and human subjectivity. Such an endeavour is evident in his rejection of economism, his more sophisticated appreciation of the relationship between ideology and consciousness, his wider appraisal of the autonomy of the state, and his novel interpretation of the role of intellectuals in the class struggle.

It is pertinent to note that a Merrington has noted, the starting point for Gramsci's work can be found in his explicit rejection of economism (Merrington, 1978). For Gramsci, the variant of Marxism espoused by Kautsky and Plekhanov, in attempting to develop a pseudo-science capable of predicting the volatile forces of capitalism, had neglected the most crucial feature of the dialectical approach: the interplay between the objective and subjective in the historical process. In so doing, it had reduced the complexity of the superstructure, the role of the political, the ideological and the cultural, to the status of mere emanations of the economic base (Merrington, 1977, p. 143).

This is often referred to as the base/superstructure model in which the state is denied autonomy, and can be understood only in terms of its function of reproducing the relations of production, the relationship of exploitation between the proletariat and the bourgeoisie. In this context, Gramsci argued that economism was not only unable to account for important political events such as the rise of Fascism in Italy, or the increasing importance of Catholicism, but was incapable of grasping the complexity of the class struggle itself (Gramsci, 1971, pp. 158-85). However, as Merrington has noted, the key to understanding Gramsci's theoretical originality lies in the fact that the private ownership of the means of production is a necessary, but not a sufficient basis, for capitalist domination (Merrington, 1977, p. 144).

If we are to understand the complexity of any particular conjuncture, then it is essential, in Gramsci's opinion, to examine the political, the cultural and the ideological dimensions of class struggle. Thus, while he was willing to concede that the basic course of human history is explained by the development of the forces of production, he was also eager to emphasise that its trajectory would be shaped in accordance with the particular circumstances of each country.

For Gramsci, then, historical change cannot be understood in terms of a simple linear development

(Communism inevitably follows capitalism), but should be appreciated in all its complexity. It is open and contingent and there are crucial political, ideological and cultural dimensions to the development of consciousness. 'Consciousness' here refers to more than the economic experience of exploitation; it involves an understanding of how people are subjected to the effects of competing ideological views of the world. Before Gramsci, the problem of order within Marxism had been explained in terms of force, repression or the overpowering dominance of bourgeois ideology. In the *German Ideology,* for example, Marx and Engels argued that the ideas of the ruling class were in every historical period the ruling ideas and that the class which is the ruling material force in society is at the same time its ruling intellectual force (Marx, 1845).

In developing the concept of hegemony, Gramsci's position deviated from that of Marx and Engels in two important respects. First, Gramsci emphasised the grave importance of ideological superstructures *vis-a-vis* the economic structure (the autonomy of the state). Second, his views on hegemony display an important emphasis on the role of consent within civil society as opposed to the use of pure force by the state. According to Gramsci, the rule of a particular class contains two separate dimensions: coercion (dominance), and social-moral leadership. Hegemony refers to the way that class domination is based not simply upon coercion but upon the cultural and ideological acquiescence of subordinate classes. The political cannot therefore be understood as either force or consent: it is both force *and* consent. In this context, a class may be deemed to be hegemonic only when it has gained the active consent of the subordinate class. Consent, here, should not be understood to be a permanent state of affairs, rather it conveys the impression of a struggle between competing ideological positions that are shifting constantly to 'accommodate the changing nature of historical circumstances and the demands and reflexive actions of human beings.'

Notably, the concept of hegemony is crucial to Gramsci's theoretical framework, since its aim is to redefine the nature of power in modern society; and to attribute a greater degree of importance to the struggle taking place at the ideological, political and cultural levels. However, although Gramsci was eager to emphasise the autonomy of the superstructure, he nevertheless recognised that it was intimately connected to the relations of production. Although hegemony is ethical-political, 'it must also be economic, must necessarily be based on the decisive function exercised by the leading group in the decisive nucleus of economic activity'. The concept of the state assumes a wider and more organic sense in Gramsci's work, an alternative arena for struggle, with a corresponding increase in the level of importance attached to its role and function in modem society. Thus Gramsci argues that the state consists of the 'entire complex of political and theoretical activities with which the ruling class not only justifies and maintains its dominance, but manages to win the active consent of those over whom it rules.'

Basically, the conception of power is extended to include a vast array of institutions through which power relations are mediated in society: education, the mass media, parliaments and courts, are all 'activities and initiatives which form the apparatus of the political and cultural hegemony of the ruling classes' (Gramsci, 1971, p. 258). The increasing importance accorded to the state in Gramsci's work is evidenced by the fact that he considered the struggle

Over consciousness to be as important as the struggle over the ownership of the means of production (Carnoy, 1984, p. 75).

It is not simply an issue of the experience of exploitation, bur how subordinate classes receive competing ideological interpretations of that reality. For Gramsci, the political struggle of the class and party was undertaken with the specific aim of establishing an alternative hegemony and, by implication, the political struggle needs to embrace the ideological, cultural and moral currents of society.

Within this wider, organic sense of struggle, Gramsci assigns an increasing level of importance to the role of the intellectuals. As he observed, there is no organisation without intellectuals, and therefore the political unity of any revolutionary organisation required a corresponding level of ideological coherence, in which the party, the intellectuals and the masses are brought into an organic relationship (Gramsci, 1971, p. 334). This issue, which revolves essentially around how the unity between the economic structure and the superstructure is achieved, occupied the central theme in *Southern Question* (1971).

As with other areas of Grasp work, the objective was to unmask the complexity of the concrete situation: (conjuncture), to examine the terrain of political struggle and inform the activity of the party (Showstack-Sassoon, 1987, p. 180). Crucially for Gramsci, theory could not 'be the result of a rationalistic, deductive, abstract process . . . one typical of pure intellectuals', but a process that is verified only in relation to political practice.

Notably, the central thrust of Gramsci's work, then, was to reassert the role of the subject within Marxism. As such, his work is dominated by a more systematic appreciation of the role of ideology, the capitalist state and a rejection of abstract theory. The tradition of French structuralism, which rose to prominence in the 1960s and 1970s, is diametrically opposed to this position. As its critics have often noted, structuralism is a theoretical tradition bereft of a subjective core. There are no subjects in history as structuralism formulates it, only individuals who occupy objective structures.

Nicos Poulantzas

Remarkably, from the outset it is important to recognise that Poulantzas's theoretical position shifted dramatically between the publication of *Political Power and Social Classes* (1974) and *State Power and Socialism* (1978) as he sought to remove the structuralist residues of his earlier publications. However, in a number of important respects, Poulantzas's later views on the capitalist state still owe a great deal to the influence of? French structuralism, **and** in particular, the work of Louis Althusser.

This was most visible in his rejection of economism, his sustained commitment to the concept of relative autonomy, and his belief that history could not be understood in terms of a linear form of development (historicism)." In the opening statements of *State Power and Socialism* Poulantzas presents a crucial paradox for contemporary state theory. It is obvious, he argues, that we are 'hemmed in more tightly by a state whose most detailed practices demonstrate its connection with particular, and extremely precise, interests' and yet at the same time 'while the bourgeoisie continue to derive many benefits from such a state, it is by no means always contented with it.' Adopting Althusser's concept of relative autonomy, Poulantzas argued that if the capitalist state was to function successfully as a class state, acting in the long-term interests of the bourgeoisie, then it must retain a degree of autonomy from the dominant class.

As Jessop notes; the exclusion of any open class bias enables the capitalist state to present itself not as a class state, a state for particular interests, but as a state operating in the interests of the general public (people-nation) (Jessop, 1985, p. 68). As Poulantzas points out, in the process of securing class hegemony, the create 'acts within an unstable equilibrium' of compromises between the dominant classes and the dominated 'and as such may adopt measures which are of a positive benefit to the masses' (Poulantzas, 1978, pp. 31, 127-45). Yet, while Poulantzas accepts fully Althusser's view that the political and ideological levels are relatively autonomous, he is at pains to stress that this is because the political and ideological levels are 'already present in the actual constitution of the relations of production that they play such an essential role in their reproduction'. In other words, the role of the political and ideological is not limited to reproducing the external conditions in which production takes place; rather, it is a crucial component in the social relations of production. For Poulantzas, the capitalist form of production involves inherently a process of class identification and class struggle. If these relationships are to be reproduced it is imperative to see that the state plays an extended role. It is not concerned simply with the negative function of ideological mystification, but is actively involved in the positive reproduction of the capitalist production process. This is a significant step forward from the position held by Althusser.

As Poulantzas noted, as far as Althusser was concerned, the state:

> acts and functions through repression and ideological inculcation and *nothing else*. It assumes the State's efficacy

> lies in what it forbids, rules out . . . according to this conception, the economic is an instance capable of self-reproduction and self-regulation, in which the State serves merely to lay down the negative rules of the economic game. (Poulantzas, 1978, p. 30)

According to Poulantzas, capitalism has promoted the view of democracy, 'one person one vote', as a sufficient condition for a mass democratic society. In so doing, it has displaced the struggle from the economic to the political sphere. This is a crucial theme within Poulantzas's later work, since this forms part of a process in which class subjects are atomised into individual juridicial subjects, thereby diffusing the potential for conflict between classes.

This process of (individualisation) serves not only 'to mask and obscure class relations (the capitalist State never presents itself as a class State) but also plays an active part in the divisions and isolation of the popular masses' (Poulantzas, 1978, p. 66). In addition, Poulantzas identifies the division between mental and manual labour, the role of bourgeois law and the people-nation as crucial themes in this process of reproducing atomised individuals. For Poulantzas, capitalist production is characterised by a social division of labour in which intellectual work is separated from manual work, a separation of technology from work and the use of science to rationalise power. The framework of state apparatuses, in Poulantzass opinion, rests on the permanent exclusion of the masses who are subjected to manual labour. In this way, the state not only has an important hold on the generation of new knowledge but also on how that knowledge is used (Carnoy, 1984).

Within Poulantzas's work on bourgeois law there are two distinct themes. In the first of these, and in contrast to the notion of consent within Gramsci's work, Poulantzas is not averse to stressing the repressive element of law. He argues, for example, that 'law is the code of organised public violence' (Poulantzas, 1978, p. 77) and that the state 'has a monopoly of legitimate physical violence.'

However, there is also a second distinctive theme to Poulantzas's views on the law, in which its function is to reproduce individual political subjects by presenting their unity in the people-nation (Poulantzas, 1978, p. 87). Once again, it is a process that serves to obscure class relations and avert political crisis. In this context, Poulantzas argues that, 'confronted by the struggle of the working class in the political arena, capitalist law, as it were, damps down and channels political crises, in such a way that they do not lead to a crisis of the State itself.

Within this theoretical framework, bourgeois law performs the dual function of legitimising the dispossession of the worker from the means of production, and reunifying systematically the subject under the umbrella of the people-nation. For Poulantzas, the state is actively involved in constructing both unity and disunity. It reproduces atomised individuals as juridicial subjects (preventing the unity which emerges in class-based relations of production), and reconstructs unify within the concept of the people-nation (Poulantzas, 1978, pp. 93-120).

While a large part of *State Power and Socialism* details the processes by which the stare reproduces individuals as juridicial subjects, the most significant contribution of this text is to develop a view of the state as an arena of class struggle. Thus, for Poulantzas, it is impossible to understand the form and function of the state without including its role in mediating class conflict. Moreover, while the state may act in the long-term political interests of a dominant class fraction, this does not preclude the presence of the popular classes in the stare.

As Poulantzas argues:

> The State apparatuses consecrate and reproduce hegemony by bringing the power bloc and certain dominated classes into a variable game of provisional compromises. The State apparatuses organise and unify the dominant power bloc by permanently disorganising — dividing the dominated classes. (Poulantzas, 1978, p. 140)

Notably, this later work does not simply emphasise the presence of conflict over state power, but rather stresses the fact that this conflict takes place within the institutional apparatus of the state itself. Here, the state is presented as a fractured polity, riven with contradictions and divisions. The different branches or sectors of the state act as power centres for different class fractions or alliances within the dominant power bloc. It is in this sense that the state is perceived as a strategic field, site, terrain or process of interconnecting power networks (Poulantzas, 1978, p. 132).

For Poulantzas, the often chaotic and incoherent nature of state policy is attributable to the way in which the struggle between different class fractions is mediated by the institutions of the state. Here, Poulantzas identifies a process of structural selectivity that consists of a set of institutional mechanisms which serve to advance or obstruct (filter) the strategies of particular class fractions.

To sum up, then, Poulantzas's work reflects the development and transformation of a structuralist view of the state into one that is more historically specific, where social movements play a key role. There are two crucial themes embodied in this position. First, the capitalist state and the relations of production have undergone significant change and can only be understood as being historically specific, or associated with a particular stage in the development of a mode of production. Second, there has been a displacement of class struggle from production into the heart of the state.

The forms and functions of the state are not determined by the class struggle in some abstract sense, but are the historical expression of those relations in the form of struggle (Carnoy, 1984). Within this conception of the state as a strategic terrain, state policy is explained in terms of strategic causality, a process involving strategic calculation without individual calculating subjects. Although the concept of relative autonomy was crucial to Poulantzas's theoretical framework its function and meaning shifted considerably between the publication of *Political Power and Social Classes* (1974) and *State Power and Socialism* (1978) (Jessop, 1985).

In his earlier work, the concept referred to the level of institutional autonomy required to organise the unity of the dominant class fraction (s) in order to secure their hegemony over the nation-people (Jessop, 1985, p. 132). Here, the crucial question is, as his critics have pointed out, 'How relative is the relative autonomy of the state?' In reply, Poulantzas argued that

> the degree, the extent, the forms, etc (how relative, and how is it relative) of the relative autonomy of the State can only be examined . . . with reference to a given capitalist State, and to the precise conjuncture of the corresponding class struggle . . . I cannot, therefore, answer this question in its general form precisely on account of the conjuncture of the class struggle, (cited in Jessop, 1985, p. 134)

As Jessop observes, there is an explicit tension here between necessity and contingency in relating institutional forms and the class struggle. Put simply, while Poulantzas wanted to avoid the charge of economic reductionism, by introducing an element of contingency, he did not want to abandon the Marxian view that the capitalist state must, in the long run, reproduce bourgeois class domination (Jessop, 1985, p. 134). In his later work, the unity of the state is no longer seen in terms of the functional imperative of reproducing class domination.

Instead, Poulantzas argues that the long-term political interest of the bourgeoisie emerges as a result of a multiplicity of diversified micro-policies which reflect the nature of class struggle. However, as Jessop notes, this does not provide an adequate solution to the problem, since Poulantzas would need to address the awkward issue of how this macroscopic necessity (the need to ensure bourgeois class domination) emerges out of microscopic diversity (the chaotic nature of state policies). More disturbing, perhaps, is the fact that had Poulantzas been successful in identifying how the relative autonomy of the state ensured class hegemony, it would have undermined his view that crises of hegemony occur.

Since the publication of *State Power and Socialism* the emphasis has shifted as the status of class analysis within the Marxist tradition has come under closer scrutiny. Authors such as Jessop now emphasise the role of desaggregation in social analysis; the importance of avoiding essentialist forms of explanation; and the need to address the role of calculating subjects within the state apparatus (state autonomy/strategy).

Thus, within Jessop's work, the tension between necessity and contingency in relating institutional forms and the class struggle has been resolved by a tendency to abandon the primary role accorded to class struggle (particularly the role of the proletariat) in favour of a wider, more flexible conception of struggle which acknowledges the need to disaggregate social analysis and embrace the particularities of divisions along the lines of gender and ethnicity.

The most important area of concern within contemporary Marxist theory of the state involves the continuing dialogue over the rejection of economism. In general terms, there has been a concerted move away from economism, retreating from the primacy of the economic within social analysis and, in turn, embracing an approach that stresses the dialectical and contingent quality of relationships. This tendency perhaps finds its most complete expression in the work of Jessop, who insists upon the multiplicity of possible causal mechanisms or principles of explanation' and refuses to 'privilege economic determinations in the "first, intermediate or last instance.' It is is important to recognise that while Jessop insists upon the multiplicity of determinations, and refuses to privilege any (single) point of reference, he does not rule out causal explanation, provided that causality is conceived in terms of contingent necessity.

Thus Jessop states that While a combination or interaction of different causal chains produces a determinate outcome (necessity), there is no single theory that can predict or determine the manner in which such causal chains converge and/or interact (contingency)' (Jessop, 1982, p. 224).

Within Jessop's frame of reference there is explicit recognition of the need to disaggregate social analysis. Moreover, as Jessop acknowledges explicitly, the interests of capital in general cannot be identified outside the framework of historically specific accumulation strategies.

However, in at least one important respect, Jessop's work differs significantly from that of B. Hindess and P. Hirst because, while he is unwilling to privilege the economic dimension within social analysis, his work at both empirical and theoretical levels appreciates that a correspondence between the state and the economy, understood in terms of the need for reproduction, is a possibility, but that it must be constructed in the course of a struggle.

For Jessop, any attempt to conceptualise the relationship between the state and civil society faces the difficulty involved in distinguishing between instrumentalism and structuralism in relation to economism. The instrumentalist position assumes that the state is a neutral institutional ensemble accessible to all political forces equally, and that it is capable of possessing a variety of objectives and goals. In contrast, a structuralist approach equates the nature, form and the activities of the state with the basic structures of the economy.

The emphasis within the structuralist tradition is on the constraints to which the state is subject in a capitalist society and the claim that, irrespective of the views of state managers, policies will be designed to ensure the continued reproduction of capital. Jessop's contention is that both approaches contain debilitating weaknesses. If one accords the state a form of neutrality and thus views it as unbiased in its effects on the interest realisation of different social forces, one is forced to explain the nature, form and the policies of the state purely in terms of those who are in control. In contrast, structuralism seeks to explain the form of the state, its functions and modes of intervention in terms of determining structures, the needs of which must be met to some degree or another. At the most general level of abstraction, Jessop detects within capitalism a number of key defining characteristics. Primarily, it involves a basic circuit of capital and a fundamental social relationship: the value form (capital/wage labour relationship).

However, the exact nature of that circuit of capital, the specific operation of the value form and the relationship between them, must be understood as being problematical and historically specific. In Jessop's view, then, although it is impossible to understand capitalism without reference to the complexities of the value form, the value form itself does not determine fully the course of capital accumulation.

Indeed, the very substance of value depends on capital's ability to control wage labour, a process that is, in turn, contingent upon a struggle shaped and moulded by factors beyond the confines of the value form. Jessop's treatment of the state and the extent to which it pushes forward the interests of capital reflects this indeterminism. He regards the interests of capital, the unity of the state and the relationship between capital and the stare as being problematical. Following Poulantzas (1978), Jessop stresses the need to distinguish between capital in general and particular forms of capital. Jessop concedes that there are necessary interests Which capital in general must realise if capitalism is to be reproduced. However, there is an extensive array of problems and contradictions which question whether these aims can be achieved successfully.

Thus, while Jessop would concede that a correspondence between the state and economic region is possible, he is at pains to stress that it is a correspondence which must always be constituted in the course of dialectical struggle, the outcome of which is always in question. For Jessop, the state consists of a plurality of institutions with no pre-given unity and no necessary relationship to the capitalist mode of production and/or the economically dominant class (Jessop, 1982, p. 222).

State power may be deemed to be capitalist only to the extent that it either creates, 'maintains or restores the conditions required for capital accumulation within a given situation' (Jessop, 1982, p. 221). While he recognises that the state may, and indeed possibly *will,* enjoy autonomy, the extent of that autonomy must be explained.

It is crucial to recognise, therefore, that political and economic forces are themselves shaped by the institutional structures and effects of state intervention; thus relations between the state and the social relations of production are always reciprocal and dialectical. Within such a theoretical arrangement, state power is conceived as being a complex social relationship which at any given time reflects the particular balance of social forces.

Hence, both the relationship between classes and that between class and non-class forces, particularly gender and ethnic divisions, are a basis of economic, social and political domination. Jessop's framework attempts systematically to remove the economically reductionist and functionalist overtones associated with the work of Poulantzas.

For Jessop, the basic contradictions involved in the circuit of capital and the value form ensure periodic crises of capital accumulation. The possibility that the capitalist class inevitably enjoys the unity essential to sustain these contradictions is opposed vehemently. Such unity can be constructed only through struggle. Moreover, it is a unity that cannot be developed in any simple form by the state, given that the state itself does not possess any essential unity.

Accordingly, Jessop does not assign to the state any form of innate power, rather:

> The State is a social relation, State power is a form determined condensation of the balance of political forces . . . the State as such has no power, it is merely an institutional ensemble: the power of the State is the power of the forces acting within the State.

Notably, should not be taken to imply that Jessop views the state as a neutral body, able to be captured and used by any social force. Rather, in Jessop's view, the state is a crucial site of struggle between social forces, the structure of which has been shaped by past struggles. In this sense, Jessop's approach begins from the simple premise that if capitalism is to be reproduced, state unity is an essential prerequisite.

His originality, lies in the emphasis he places on the way in which this unity needs actively to be constructed in and through the struggle between social forces. As such, there is no particular state form that can resolve indefinitely the inherent contradictions within relations between capital and labour. For Jessop, this means that class conflict will be reproduced at the very heart of the state apparatus. Thus, in Jessop's opinion, the effectiveness of state power depends ultimately upon the balance of forces in any given situation.

Strategies for organising a secure social base (corporatism, for example) will vary with the particular stage of development, the form of the state and the location in the world economy. This complexity necessarily means that 'blanket generalisations' are inappropriate and that it 'would be wrong to suggest that any given state form best secures an adequate social base in all situations'.

For Jessop, the state is now viewed as being a strategic terrain and the emphasis has focused increasingly on strategic considerations. Thus Jessop argues that 'The State is not simply something towards which one must adopt a political strategy but is something (or better, a social relation) which can be fruitfully analysed as the site, the generator, and the product of strategies (Jessop, 1989, p. 3).

According to this view, any theory of the state must produce an informed analysis of the strategic calculations and practices of the actors involved and of the interaction between agents and the state structures.

However, the relationship is always dynamic and dialectical; state structures effect both strategic assessments and strategic conduct, which, in turn, effect change within state structures. Not all of Jessop's work is pitched at such a high level of abstraction. Indeed, if the interests of capital in general can no longer be identified outside the framework of historically specific accumulation strategies, and there can be no ultimate state form that is able to serve as an unambiguously favourable political shell for advancing these interests, this suggests that there is no abstract theoretical solution to the question of how the political class domination of capital is secured.

The answer, in Jessop's opinion, is to be found at the level of specific conjunctures in terms of the complex interaction between the circuit of capital, accumulation strategies, state forms and the balance of political forces. A successful capitalist state is one which has a unified form with a strategic selectivity that privileges the bourgeoisie. It is unified through a hegemonic project incorporating political, ideological and economic aspects which legitimise the dominance of the capitalist class, or more probably one fraction of it, over other social forces. Within such theorising there exists a tension between, on the one hand, recognising the possibility of a correlation between an effective accumulation strategy and a successful hegemonic project and, on the other, the theoretical need to question the likelihood of such an occurrence, given the mass of contradictions among possible strategic options and the nature of strategic conduct involved in the operation of capitalism.

Even so, Jessop's primary concern is with empirical regularity, involving a correspondence between an effective accumulation strategy *and* a successful hegemonic project. As the previous remarks imply, there can be no macro-necessity in social relations and as a result we must reject on principle the notion that somehow there is a totality 'out there' which remains fixed and constant. Jessop rejects the possibility of any comprehensive or complete strategy, because this would presuppose either the presence of a global subject, omnipresent and omnipotent, or some form of super-determination. There is never just a single calculating subject; rather, we are faced with a plurality of calculating subjects and a plethora of competing and contradictory strategies.

The totality is thus conceptualised as possessing no determining centre or inner essence. There are no universal or unifying strategies. Strategies are always particular, relational, relative and conjunctural. They present themselves only as possible methods in which to organise and articulate a number of smaller sites of power and/or agents (Jessop, 1989). (For reasons of space it is not possible to discuss Jessop's recent embrace of a modified form of Regulation Theory.

Contemporary variants of the Marxist theory of the state have therefore not gone uncriricised. Authors from a wide variety of perspectives have argued that the transformation of the post-war economies, the entrenchment of the welfare state and the threat posed by environmental degradation have all questioned the pivotal role accorded to the concept of class within the Marxist framework. The remaining sections of this chapter explore briefly the core themes of such critical postures, focusing on the contentious issue of state autonomy an the challenge presented by the environmentalist and feminist traditions.

Fred Block and Theda Skocpol

The work of Block and Skocpol is related, although Block retains more Marxist residues than does Skocpol. As the title of Skocpol's essay suggests (Skocpol, 1985) the accent within American political theory in the last two decades has been to focus upon the specificity of the state, its institutional autonomy and its capacity as an actor to realise policy goals. The objective within this particular variant of state theory has been been to reject the grand' theorising of structuralism and produce 'solidly grounded and analytically sharp understandings of the causal regularities that underlie the histories of states' (Skocpol, 1985, p. 28).

Thus Skocpol argues that the state should be seen as both an organisation through which an official collectivity may pursue distinctive goals and as a set of institutions which influence the meanings and methods of politics. Consequently, structuralism is charged with the failure to address adequately the idea of stare autonomy and the importance of state actors in realising specific policy goals (Skocpol, 1985, p. 28). As emphasised. Block's work retains strong Marxist residues, but he rejects the concept of relative autonomy because it assumes that the ruling class has 'some degree of political cohesion, an understanding of its general interests, and a high degree of political sophistication'. Instead, Block suggests that the starting point for analysis should be the division of labour between those who accumulate capital and those who manage the state apparatus.

Within this division of labour. Block contends that capitalists are only conscious of the specific short-term economic interests of their firms and are unaware of how to ensure the reproduction of the social order. Accordingly, attention needs to be diverted towards the crucial function of state managers (calculating subjects) in reproducing the conditions for sustained economic growth. In this context there are two themes that need to be addressed. First, we need to explain the structural constraints that reduce the likelihood that state managers will oppose the interests of business. Second, it is necessary to explain why state managers may actually extend state power, even in the face of capitalist resistance (Block, 1977, p. 7). Within Block's theoretical position, the capacity of capitalism to rationalise itself is no longer viewed as being the sole responsibility of the capitalist class, but is the outcome of a conflict between the capitalist class, the managers of the state apparatus and the working class.

For Block, the problem is one of how to explain the tendency of the state to serve the interests of the dominant class without succumbing to the problems of instrumentalist or functionalist forms of explanation. Block's response is to suggest that the placement of members of the dominant class in key positions within the state is an insufficient basis for reproducing capitalism, because: for one thing, ruling class members who devote substantial energy to policy formation become atypical of their class, since they are forced to look at the world from the perspective of managers. They are quite likely to diverge from ruling class opinion. (Block 1977, p. 13)

Block's preference is to view state managers as collectively self-interested maximisers who have interests that are linked to the specific needs of continued economic growth. This does not assume that state managers are capable of resolving the problems of capitalism, or producing the most favourable responses to crisis; rather, it conveys the idea that the actions of state managers are taken within the constraints imposed by political realities and economic orthodoxies.

The Challenge of Feminism and Environmentalism

For Marxists, the appeal of the concept of class rests on the dual function it performs as both a descriptive category and an explanatory variable. In this sense it is possible both to assign people to a particular class (bourgeibsie/proletariat), and to suggest that this will influence a particular form of political behaviour. Such arguments have, in the 1990s, been roundly condemned by elements within both feminist and environmentalist traditions, on the grounds that they are either 'sex blind' or neglect to consider one of the most pressing problem facing society: environmental degradation.

From the outset, it is important to recognise a wide variety of position within both the environmentalist (see Eckersly, 1992) and feminist traditions (see Humm, 1992). For authors such as Hartmann, recent attempts to integrate Marxism and feminism have proved unsatisfactory because they have subsumed the feminist struggle into the larger struggle against capital (Hartmann, 1992). Consequently, many of the weaknesses in Marxism, such as economism or the way in which it has homogenised class interests, has prevented it from theorising adequately on the position of women and other non-class oppressions.

Here the principal objection is that Marxist categories are rooted in relations of appropriation and exploitation which fail to consider the particular gender of the exploiters and those whose labour is appropriated (Barrett, 1992). In contrast, a great deal of contemporary radical feminism now concentrates upon the 'particularities of women's lives', or the specific identity around which a feminist struggle can be sustained (Segal, 1991, p. 280). It is a position which replaces the central role accorded to the 'relations of production' within Marxist theory with an exploration of consciousness-raising or, as Mackinnon prefers, the 'collective critical reconstitution of the meaning of women's social experience, as women live through it' (Mackinnon, 1992, p. 119).

For the more radical variants of feminism, then, Marxist categories are inappropriate to an adequate understanding of the ideology of familialsim, particular forms of household organisation, sexuality and male power that are crucial to the subjugation of women under capitalism.

In a similar fashion, the environmentalist movement has sought to challenge the economic orthodoxy of Marxist theory: the all-pervasive role of class druggie, its reliance upon a productivist ethos and the continued domination of nature by humanity. Accordingly, Marxist theory is charged with possessing an intellectual legacy that is incompatible with current environmental concerns.

For authors such as Gorz, there is now a myriad of antagonisms superimposed upon the contradiction between capital and labour. It is no longer possible, therefore, to answer the question of who will perform the crucial function of carrying out the socialist revolution by means of traditional class analysis (Gorz, 1991, p. 289). Within this critique, two themes are sythesised: a rejection of the role accorded to the working class in the socialist project, and the need to embrace an environmentally-informed vision of society that emphasises the *limitations to* economic growth (Gorz, 1980, 1982).

For Gorz, the subject of a socialist project can no longer be found in the capitalist/wage labour nexus but must be located in the worker (as citizen) who is confronted by the imperfections of modern capitalism (Gorz, 1982). Thus, Gorz states that where socialism understands itself as the 'planned development of not yet existing economic structures . . . it reconstructs a society so that it is devoted to the economic development of capital accumulation' (Gorz, 1991, p. 289). The most pressing problem for Marxism, then, is that it is rooted ultimately in a conception of society that neglects to consider one of the most serious problem facing society: ecological degradation.

To sum up Among those authors who retain allegiance to the Left it has become an accepted practice to replace the role of class struggle with an amalgam of metaphors designed to invoke a wider, more flexible appreciation of the disparate elements involved within the socialist project. It is now more commonplace, for example, to argue in terms of 'alternative sites of struggle', or to emphasise the importance of social movements.

This trend, which is now firmly entrenched, has occurred largely as a result of a systematic attempt to rid Marxism of essentialist or reductionist forms of explanation in favour of concepts which stress the partially contingent nature of social reality. This represents a crucial departure, since it also rejects the view that society inevitably follows a particular path, and that class struggle inevitably leads to the 'end' of history.

The instrumentalist concern with who rules the state has been abandoned firmly in favour of an approach which argues either that the class nature of the state is expressed through the 'structure' of capitalist development, or chat the state is a political apparatus through which control is contested between the dominant/subordinate classes and social movements.

Communism. Such theoretical developments have been influenced by rapid changes taking place within capitalism: the transformation of work relations, the growth of the Keynesian welfare state and the decline of trade union power - all of which appear to have combined to sound the death knell for class politics, ensuring that the central role for the working class in the struggle for socialism can no longer be guaranteed. Within such work, the rise of environmental and feminist protest groups represents a potential new source around which to form a political struggle, one in which a 'broad church' or 'rainbow alliance' of eco-feminist-socialist groups has the potential to transform society. Such developments have had an important bearing upon contemporary Marxist theory of the state. Few authors are now willing to defend a universal theory of the state, rather, they propose specific historical analysis within a universalistic conception of the relationship between the stare and economy.

6

Democratic Peace Theory

> "A fair amount of gripping is a wonderful thing. It is healthy and a good way to let off steam. Dissatisfaction with the status quo leads to improvements and then we have."
>
> —*Stephen Baker*

First it is remarkable to note that democratic peace theory (or liberal democratic theory or simply the democratic peace) holds that democracies, for some appropriate definition of democracy, rarely go to war with one another.

Generally, it is seen that the wording "democratic peace theory" is often disputed since, even if the theory is accepted, it does not imply that the "peace" has the key characteristics of a "democracy" among countries. Some critics argue that it will be more accurate to label it the "democracies do not fight each other" hypothesis.

In fact, the original theory and research on wars has been followed by many similar theories and related research on the relationship between democracy and peace, including that lesser conflicts than wars are also rare between democracies, and that systematic violence is in general less common within democracies.

History

Now about the emergence and growth of the theory. Although the philosophical idea has circulated since Immanuel Kant, it was not scientifically evaluated until the 1960s. Kant foreshadowed the theory in his essay *Perpetual Peace* written in 1795, although he thought that constitutional republics was only one of several necessary conditions for a perpetual peace. Kant's theory was that a majority of the people would never vote to go to war, unless in self defense.

Therefore, if all nations were republics, it would end war, because there would be no aggressors. Other explanations have been proposed since, but the modern theory is principally the empirical claim that democracies rarely or never fight (Ray 1998). Dean Babst, a criminologist, was the first to do statistical research on this topic. He wrote an academic paper supporting the theory in 1964 in *Wisconsin Sociologist*; he published a slightly more popularized version, in 1972, in the trade journal *Industrial Research*. Both versions initially received little attention. Melvin Small and J. David Singer (1976: 50—69) responded; they found an absence of wars between democratic states with two "marginal exceptions", but denied that this pattern had statistical significance, starting the academic debate. This paper was published in the *Jerusalem Journal of International Relations* which finally brought more widespread attention to the theory, as did Michael Doyle's (1983) lengthy discussion of the topic. Rudolph J. Rummel was another early researcher and drew considerable lay attention to the subject in his later works.

Maoz & Abdolali (1989) extended the research to lesser conflicts than wars. Bremer (1992) and Maoz & Russett (1993) found the correlation between democracy and peacefulness remained significant after controlling for many possible confounding variables. This moved the theory into the mainstream of social science. Supporters of Realism in international relations and others responded by raising many new objections. Other researchers attempted more systematic explanations of how democracy might cause peace (Köchler 1995), and of how democracy might also affect other aspects of foreign relations such as alliances and collaboration (Ray 2003).

There have been numerous further studies in the field since these pioneering works. Most studies have found some form of democratic peace exists, although neither methodological disputes nor doubtful cases are entirely resolved (Kinsella 2005).

Key Terms

Research on the democratic peace theory has to define "democracy" and "peace" (or, more often, "war"). Similarly, the main criticism contends that the theory is an example of equivocation, particularly, No true Scotsman fallacy.

Democracy

Democracies have been defined differently by different theorists and researchers; this accounts for some of the variations in their findings. Some examples: Kant (1795) opposed direct democracy since it is "necessarily despotism, as it establishes an executive power contrary to the general will; all being able to decide against one whose opinion may differ, the will of all is therefore not that of all: which is contradictory and opposite to liberty." Instead, Kant favors a constitutional republic where individual liberty is protected from the will of the majority.

Small and Singer (1976) define democracy as a nation

that (1) holds periodic elections in which the opposition parties are as free to run as government parties, (2) allows at least 10% of the adult population to vote, and (3) has a parliament that either controls or enjoys parity with the executive branch of the government.

Further, Doyle (1983) requires (1) that "liberal régimes" have market or private property economics, (2) they have polities that are externally sovereign, (3) they have citizens with juridical rights, and (4) they have representative governments. Either 30% of the adult males were able to vote or it was possible for every man to acquire voting rights as by attaining enough property. He allows greater power to hereditary monarchs than other researchers; for example, he counts the rule of Louis-Philippe of France as a liberal régime. Ray (1995) requires that at least 50% of the adult population is allowed to vote and that there has been at least one peaceful, constitutional transfer of executive power from one independent political party to another by means of an election. Rummel (1997) states that "By democracy is meant liberal democracy, where those who hold power are elected in competitive elections with a secret ballot and wide franchise (loosely understood as including at least 2/3rds of adult males); where there is freedom of speech, religion, and organization; and a constitutional framework of law to which the government is subordinate and that guarantees equal rights."

The above definitions are binary, classifying nations into either democracies or nondemocracies. Many researchers have instead used more finely grained scales. One example is the Polity data series which scores each state on two scales, one for democracy and one for autocracy, for each year since 1800; as well as several others.

The use of the Polity Data has varied. Some researchers

have done correlations between the democracy scale and belligerence; others have treated it as a binary classification by (as its maker does) calling all states with a high democracy score and a low autocracy score democracies; yet others have used the difference of the two scores, sometimes again making this into a binary classification (Gleditsch 1992).

Young Democracies

Several researchers have observed that many of the possible exceptions to the democratic peace have occurred when at least one of the involved democracies was very young. Many of them have therefore added a qualifier, typically stating that the peacefulness apply to democracies older than 3 years (Doyle 1983), (Russett 1993), (Rummel 1997), (Weart 1998). Rummel (1997) argues that this is enough time for "democratic procedures to be accepted, and democratic culture to settle in." Additionally, this may allow for other states to actually come to the recognition of the state as a democracy. Mansfield and Snyder (2002, 2005), while agreeing that there have been no wars between mature liberal democracies, state that countries in transition to democracy are especially likely to be involved in wars. They find that democratizing countries are even more warlike than stable democracies, stable autocracies or even countries in transition towards autocracy.

So, they suggest caution in eliminating these wars from the analysis, because this might hide a negative aspect of the process of democratization. A reanalysis of the earlier study's statistical results (Braumoeller 2004) emphasizes that the above relationship between democratization and war can only be said to hold for those democratizing countries where the executive lacks sufficient power, independence, and institutional strength.

A review (Ray 2003) cites several other studies finding that the increase in the risk of war in democratizing countries happens only if many or most of the surrounding nations are undemocratic. If wars between young democracies are included in the analysis, several studies and reviews still find enough evidence supporting the stronger claim that all democracies, whether young or established, go into war with one another less frequently (Ray 1998), (Ray 2003), (Hegre 2004), while some do not (Schwartz & Skinner 2002).

Economic Peace Theory

A derivative of the democratic peace theory that a semi-autonomous territory uses to ameliorate a potential occupying power's aggression through increased economic exchange in the hopes that these efforts will lead to political results. The whole relationship between the newly elected president of Taiwan Ma Ying Jeou and Chinese president Hu Jintao negotiating increased economic exchange through their respective representative bodies SEF and ARATS is contingent upon this theory.

Wars and Lesser Conflicts

Quantitative research on international wars usually define war as a military conflict with more than 1000 killed in battle. This is the definition used in the Correlates of War Project which has also supplied the data for many studies on war. It turns out that most of the military conflicts in question fall clearly above or below this threshold (Ray 1995, p. 103). Some researchers have used different definitions. For example, Weart (1998) defines war as more than 200 battle deaths. Russett (1993, p. 50), when looking at Ancient Greece, only requires some real battle engagement, involving on both sides forces under state authorization. Militarized Interstate Disputes (MIDs), in the Correlates of War Project classification, are lesser conflicts than wars. Such a conflict may be no more than military display of force with no battle deaths. MIDs and wars together are "militarized interstate conflicts" or MICs. MIDs include the conflicts that precede a war; so the difference between MIDs and MICs may be less than it appears.

Statistical analysis and concerns about degrees of freedom are the primary reasons for using MID's instead of actual wars. Wars are relatively rare. An average ratio of 30 MIDs to one war provides a richer statistical environment for analysis.

Monadic vs. Dyadic Peace

Most research is regarding the *dyadic* peace, that democracies do not fight one another. Very few researchers have supported the *monadic* peace, that democracies are more peaceful in general. There are some recent papers that find a slight monadic effect. Müller and Wolff (2004), in listing them, agree "that democracies on average might be slightly, but not strongly, less warlike than other states," but general "monadic explanations is neither necessary nor convincing". They note that democracies have varied greatly in their belligerence against non-democracies.

Historically, cases commonly cited as exceptions include the Spanish-American War, the Continuation War and more recently the Kargil War.

Some theorists cite these or other exceptions, but nevertheless regard them as marginal cases.

Rebuttals

Advocates of the theory who describe war between

democracies only as "rare", "very rare", "rare or non-existent" account for the possibility of a very few or marginal exceptions, while undercutting their significance.

Some advocates also minimize the significance of any exceptions by stating the theory in a probabilistic form: since such a very great many wars have been fought since democracies first arose, we might expect some proportionately large number of wars to have occurred between democracies; however the historical record reveals this number to be either at or near zero, depending on interpretation, with the finding that no wars at all have taken place between well-established liberal democracies being common. One review (Ray 1998) found that, in probabilistic terms, the correlation between democracy and peace is statistically significant. In broader terms, Jack Levy has famously characterized the strength of this correlation as being "as close as anything we have to an empirical law in international relations" (Levy 1988). Bremer (Bremer 1992, 1993), a strong advocate of the theory, notes this issue of interpretation, but questions its relevance. He argues that it is "fruitless to debate the question of whether democracies never or only very rarely fight one another," since in either case, the central insight of the theory is valid. Most researchers incline to this view (Gleditsch 1992); an exception is Rummel (Rummel 1983).

Lesser Conflicts

One problem with the research on wars is that, as the Realist Mearsheimer (1990, p. 50) put it, "democracies have been few in number over the past two centuries, and thus there have been few opportunities where democracies were in a position to fight one another". Especially if using a strict definition of democracy, as by those finding no wars.

Democracies have been very rare until recently. Even looser definitions of democracy, such as Doyle's, find only a dozen democracies before the late nineteenth century, and many of them short-lived or with limited franchise (Doyle 1983), (Doyle 1997, p. 261). Freedom House finds no independent state with universal suffrage in 1900.

Wayman (1998), a supporter of the theory, states that "If we rely solely on whether there has been an inter-democratic war, it is going to take many more decades of peace to build our confidence in the stability of the democratic peace". Many researchers reacted to this limitation by studying lesser conflicts instead, since they have been far more common. There have been many more MIDs than wars; the Correlates of War Project counts several thousand during the last two centuries. A review (Ray 2003) lists many studies that have reported that democratic pairs of states are less likely to be involved in MIDs than other pairs of states.

Another study (Hensel, Goertz & Diehl 2000) finds that after both states have become democratic, there is a decreasing probability for MIDs within a year and this decreases almost to zero within five years. When examining the inter-liberal MIDs in more detail, one study (Wayman 2002) finds that they are less likely to involve third parties, the target of the hostility is less likely to reciprocate, if the target reciprocates the response is usually proportional to the provocation, and the disputes are less likely to cause any loss of life.

The most common action was "Seizure of Material or Personnel". Studies find that the probability that disputes between states will be resolved peacefully is positively affected by the degree of democracy exhibited by the lesser democratic state involved in that dispute. Disputes between democratic states are significantly shorter than disputes involving at least one undemocratic state. Democratic states are more likely to be amenable to third party mediation when they are involved in disputes with each other (Ray 2003).

In international crises that include the threat or use of military force, one study finds that if the parties are democracies, then relative military strength has no effect on who wins. This is different from when nondemocracies are involved. These results are the same also if the conflicting parties are formal allies (Gelpi & Griesdorf 2001). Similarly, a study of the behavior of states that joined ongoing militarized disputes reports that power is important only to autocracies: democracies do not seem to base their alignment on the power of the sides in the dispute.

Conflict Initiation

Most studies have looked only at who is involved in the conflicts and ignored the question of who initiated the conflict. In many conflicts both sides argue that the other side was initiator. Several researchers, as described in (Gleditsch, Christiansen & Hegre 2004), have argued that studying conflict initiation is of limited value, because existing data about conflict initiation may be especially unreliable. Even so, several studies have examined this. Reiter and Stam (2003) argue that autocracies initiate conflicts against democracies more frequently than democracies do against autocracies.

Quackenbush and Rudy (2006), while confirming Reiter and Stam's results, find that democracies initiate wars against nondemocracies more frequently than nondemocracies do to each other. Several following studies

(Peceny & Beer 2003), (Peceny & Butler 2004), (Lai & Slater 2006) have studied how different types of autocracies with different institutions vary regarding conflict initiation.

Personalistic and military dictatorships may be particularly prone to conflict initiation, as compared to other types of autocracy such as one party states, but also more likely to be targeted in a war having other initiators.

Internal Violence and Genocide

Most of this article discusses research on relations between states. However, there is also evidence that democracies have less internal systematic violence. For instance, one study finds that the most democratic and the most authoritarian states have few civil wars, and intermediate regimes the most. The probability for a civil war is also increased by political change, regardless whether toward greater democracy or greater autocracy. Intermediate regimes continue to be the most prone to civil war, regardless of the time since the political change. In the long run, since intermediate regimes are less stable than autocracies, which in turn are less stable than democracies, durable democracy is the most probable end-point of the process of democratization (Hegre et al. 2001). Abadie (2004) study finds that the most democratic nations have the least terrorism. Harff (2003) finds that genocide and politicide are rare in democracies. Rummel (1997) finds that the more democratic a regime, the less its democide. He finds that democide has killed six times as many people as battles.

Davenport and Armstrong (2004) lists several other studies and states: "Repeatedly, democratic political systems have been found to decrease political bans, censorship, torture, disappearances and mass killing, doing so in a linear fashion across diverse measurements, methodologies, time periods, countries, and contexts." It concludes: "Across measures and methodological techniques, it is found that below a certain level, democracy has no impact on human rights violations, but above this level democracy influences repression in a negative and roughly linear manner." Davenport and Armstrong (2003) states that thirty years worth of statistical research has revealed that only two variables decrease human rights violations: political democracy and economic development.

These theories have traditionally been categorized into two groups: explanations that focus on democratic norms and explanations that focus on democratic political structures (Gelpi & Griesdorf 2001), (Braumoeller 1997). Note that they usually are meant to be explanations for little violence between democracies, not for a low level of internal violence in democracies. Several of these mechanisms may also apply to countries of similar systems. The book *Never at War* finds evidence for an oligarchic peace.

Democratic Norms

One example from the first group is that liberal democratic culture may make the leaders accustomed to negotiation and compromise (Weart 1998), (Müller & Wolff 2004). Another that a belief in human rights may make people in democracies reluctant to go to war, especially against other democracies. The decline in colonialism, also by democracies, may be related to a change in perception of non-European peoples and their rights (Ravlo & Gleditsch 2000).

Bruce Russett (1993, p. 5-11, 35, 59-62, 73-4) also argues that the democratic culture affects the way leaders resolve conflicts. In addition, he holds that a social norm emerged toward the end of the nineteenth century; that democracies should not fight each other, which strengthened when the democratic culture and the degree of democracy increased, for example by widening the franchise. Increasing democratic stability allowed partners in foreign affairs to perceive a nation as reliable democratic.

The alliances between democracies during the two World Wars and the Cold War also strengthened the norms. He sees less effective traces of this norm in Greek antiquity. Hans Köchler (1995) relates the question of transnational democracy to empowering the individual citizen by involving him, through procedures of direct democracy, in a country's international affairs, and he calls for the restructuring of the United Nations Organization according to democratic norms. He refers in particular to the Swiss practice of participatory democracy. Mousseau (2000, 2005) argues that it is market-oriented development that creates the norms and values that explain both democracy and the peace. In less developed countries individuals often depend on social networks that impose conformity to in-group norms and beliefs, and loyalty to group leaders.

When jobs are plentiful on the market, in contrast, as in market-oriented developed countries, individuals depend on a strong state that enforces contracts equally. Cognitive routines emerge of abiding by state law rather than group leaders, and, as in contracts, tolerating differences among individuals. Voters in marketplace democracies thus accept only impartial 'liberal' governments, and constrain leaders to pursue their interests in securing equal access to global markets and in resisting those who distort such access with force.

Marketplace democracies thus share common foreign policy interests in the supremacy — and predictability —

of international law over brute power politics, and equal and open global trade over closed trade and imperial preferences. When disputes do originate between marketplace democracies, they are less likely than others to escalate to violence because both states, even the stronger one, perceive greater long-term interests in the supremacy of law over power politics. Braumoeller argues that liberal norms of conflict resolution vary because liberalism takes many forms. By examining survey results from the newly-independent states of the former Soviet Union, the author demonstrates that liberalism in that region bears a stronger resemblance to 19th-century liberal nationalism than to the sort of universalist, Wilsonian liberalism described by democratic peace theorists, and that, as a result, liberals in the region are *more,* not less, aggressive than non-liberals.

Democratic Political Structures

The case for institutional constraints goes back to Kant (1795), who wrote:

> "[I]f the consent of the citizens is required in order to decide that war should be declared (and in this constitution it cannot but be the case), nothing is more natural than that they would be very cautious in commencing such a poor game, decreeing for themselves all the calamities of war. Among the latter would be: having to fight, having to pay the costs of war from their own resources, having painfully to repair the devastation war leaves behind, and, to fill up the measure of evils, load themselves with a heavy national debt that would embitter peace itself and that can never be liquidated on account of constant wars in the future"

As such, Democracy gives influence to those most likely to be killed or wounded in wars, and their relatives and friends (and to those who pay the bulk of the war taxes)

Russett (1993, p. 30). This monadic theory must, however, explain why democracies do attack non-democratic states. One explanation is that these democracies were threatened or otherwise were provoked by the non-democratic states.

Doyle (1997, p. 272) argued that the absence of a monadic peace is only to be expected: the same ideologies that cause liberal states to be at peace with each other inspire idealistic wars with the illiberal, whether to defend oppressed foreign minorities or avenge countrymen settled abroad. Doyle also notes (p. 292) liberal states do conduct covert operations against each other; the covert nature of the operation, however, prevents the publicity otherwise characteristic of a free state from applying to the question. Studies show that democratic states are more likely than autocratic states to win the wars. One explanation is that democracies, for internal political and economic reasons, have greater resources. This might mean that democratic leaders are unlikely to select other democratic states as targets because they perceive them to be particularly formidable opponents.

One study finds that interstate wars have important impacts on the fate of political regimes, and that the probability that a political leader will fall from power in the wake of a lost war is particularly high in democratic states (Ray 1998). As described in (Gelpi & Griesdorf 2001), several studies have argued that liberal leaders face institutionalized constraints that impede their capacity to mobilize the state's resources for war without the consent of a broad spectrum of interests. Survey results that compare the attitudes of citizens and elites in the Soviet successor states are consistent with this argument (Braumoeller 1997). Moreover, these constraints are readily apparent to other states and cannot be manipulated by leaders. Thus, democracies send credible signals to other states of an aversion to using force. These signals allow democratic states to avoid conflicts with one another, but they may attract aggression from nondemocratic states.

Democracies may be pressured to respond to such aggression — perhaps even preemptively — through the use of force. Also as described in (Gelpi & Griesdorf 2001), studies have argued that when democratic leaders do choose to escalate international crises, their threats are taken as highly credible, since there must be a relatively large public opinion for these actions.

In disputes between liberal states, the credibility of their bargaining signals allows them to negotiate a peaceful settlement before mobilization. An explanation based on game theory similar to the last two above is that the participation of the public and the open debate send clear and reliable information regarding the intentions of democracies to other states. In contrast, it is difficult to know the intentions of nondemocratic leaders, what effect concessions will have, and if promises will be kept.

Thus there will be mistrust and unwillingness to make concessions if at least one of the parties in a dispute is a nondemocracy (Levy & Razin 2004). The risk factors for certain types of state have, however, changed since Kant's time. In the quote above, Kant points to the lack of popular support for war - given that the populace will directly or indirectly suffer in the event of war - as a reason why republics will not tend to go to war. The number of American troops killed or maimed versus the number of Iraqi soldiers and civilians maimed and killed in the American-Iraqi conflict is indicative. This may explain the relatively great willingness of democratic states to attack weak opponents:

the Iraq war was, initially at least, highly popular in the United States.

The case of the American-Vietnamese war might, nonetheless, indicate a tipping point where publics may no longer accept continuing attrition of their soldiers (even while remaining relatively indifferent to the much higher loss of life on the part of the populations attacked).

Criticisms

There are several logically distinguishable classes of criticism. Note that they usually apply to no wars or few MIDs between democracies, not to little systematic violence in established democracies.

Only one study (Schwartz & Skinner 2002) appears to have argued that there have been as many wars between democracies as one would expect between any other couple of states. However, its authors include wars between young and dubious democracies, and very small wars.

Others (Spiro 1994), (Gowa 1999), (Small & Singer 1976) state that, although there may be some evidence for democratic peace, the data sample or the time span may be too small to assess any definitive conclusions. For example, Gowa finds evidence for democratic peace to be insignificant before 1939, because of the too small number of democracies, and offers an alternate explanation for the following period (see the section on Realist Explanations). Gowa's use of statistics has been criticized, with several other studies and reviews finding different or opposing results (Gelpi & Griesdorf 2001), (Ray 2003). However, this can be seen as the longest-lasting criticism to the theory; as noted earlier, also some supporters (Wayman 1998) agree that the statistical sample for assessing its validity is limited or scarce, at least if only full scale wars are considered. It can be interesting to consider the question of "how much" significance the evidence has. One study (Ray 2003) tries to answer this question in a straightforward way. According to Ray, who uses a rather restrictive definition of democracy and war, there have been no wars between jointly democratic couples of states in the period from 1816 to 1992.

Assuming a purely random distribution of wars between states, regardless of their democratic character, the predicted number of conflicts between democracies would be around ten. So, Ray argues that the evidence is statistically significant, but that it is still conceivable that, in the future, even a small number of inter-democratic wars wipes out such evidence.

Some authors criticize the definition of democracy by arguing that states continually reinterpret other states' regime types as a consequence of their own objective interests and motives, such as economic and security concerns (Rosato 2003). For example, one study (Oren 1995) reports that Germany was considered a democratic state by Western opinion leaders at the end of the 19th century; yet in the years preceding World War I, when its relations with the United States, France and Britain started deteriorating, Germany was gradually reinterpreted as an autocratic state, in absence of any actual regime change. Shimmin (Shimmin 1999) moves a similar criticism regarding the western perception of Milosevic's Serbia between 1989 and 1999. Rummel (Rummel 1999) replies to the above criticism by stating that, in general, studies on democratic peace do not focus on the "western" perception of democracy; and in the specific case of Serbia, by arguing that the limited credit accorded by western democracies to Milosevic in the early '90s did not amount to a recognition of democracy, but only to the perception that possible alternative leaders could be even worse. Some democratic peace researchers have been criticized for *post hoc* reclassifying some specific conflicts as non wars or political systems as non democracies without checking and correcting the whole data set used similarly. Supporters and opponents of the democratic peace agree that this is bad use of statistics, even if a plausible case can be made for the correction (Bremer 1992), (Gleditsch 1995), (Gowa 1999).

A military affairs columnist of the newspaper *Asia Times* has summarized the above criticism in a journalist's fashion describing the theory as subject to the no true Scotsman problem: exceptions are explained away as not being between *real* democracies or being *real* wars. However, most researchers agree that an objective working definition of "democracy" and "war" can be given. Even so, democracy is an evolving concept which has meant different things at different times, but in almost all cases researchers apply the same criteria to all history. Definitions of democracy that require an actual transfer of power between different political parties sometimes exclude long periods often viewed as democratic. For example, the United States until 1800, India from independence until 1979, and Japan until 1993 (Ray 1995, p. 100).

Some democratic peace researchers require that the executive result from a substantively contested election. This may be a restrictive definition: For example, the National Archives of the United States notes that "For all intents and purposes, George Washington was unopposed for election as President, both in 1789 and 1792". (Under the original provisions for the Electoral College, there was no distinction between votes for President and Vice-President: each elector was required to vote for two distinct candidates, with the runner-up to be Vice-President. Every elector cast one of his votes for Washington, John Adams received a majority of the other votes; there were several other candidates: so the election for Vice President was contested). Spiro (1994) made several other criticisms of the statistical methods used. Russett (1995) and a series of papers described by Ray (2003) responded to this, for example with different methodology.

Sometimes the datasets used have also been criticized. For example, some authors have criticized the Correlates of War data for not including civilian deaths in the battle deaths count, especially in civil wars (Sambanis 2001). Weeks and Cohen (2006) argue that most fishing disputes, which include no deaths and generally very limited threats of violence, should be excluded even from the list of military disputes.

Gleditsch (2004) made several criticisms to the Correlates of War data set, and produced a revised set of data. Maoz and Russett (1993) made several criticisms to the Polity I and II data sets, which have mostly been addressed in later versions. These criticisms are generally considered minor issues.

Political Similarity

One general criticism motivating research of different explanations is that actually the theory cannot claim that "democracy causes peace", because the evidence for democracies being, in general, more peaceful is very slight or non existent; it only can support the claim that "*joint* democracy causes peace". According to Rosato (2003), this casts doubts on whether democracy is actually the cause because, if so, a monadic effect would be expected. Perhaps the simplest explanation to such perceived anomaly (but not the one the Realist Rosato prefers, see the section on Realist explanations below) is that democracies are not peaceful to each other because they are democratic, but rather because they are *similar*.

This line of thought started with several independent observations of an "Autocratic Peace" effect, a reduced probability of war (obviously no author claims its absence) between states which are both non-democratic, or both highly so (Raknerud & Hegre 1997), (Beck & Jackman 1998), This has led to the hypothesis that democratic peace emerges as a particular case when analyzing a subset of states which are, in fact, similar (Werner 2000). Or, that similarity in general does not solely affect the probability of war, but only coherence of strong political regimes such as full democracies and stark autocracies. Autocratic peace and the explanation based on political similarity is a relatively recent development, and opinions about its value are varied. Henderson (2002) builds a model considering political similarity, geographic distance and economic interdependence as its main variables, and concludes that democratic peace is a statistical artifact which disappears when the above variables are taken into account.

Werner (2000) finds a conflict reducing effect from political similarity in general, but with democratic dyads being particularly peaceful, and noting some differences in behavior between democratic and autocratic dyads with respect to alliances and power evaluation. Beck, King and Zeng (2004) use neural networks to show two distinct low probability zones, corresponding to high democracy and high autocracy. Petersen (2004) uses a different statistical model and finds that autocratic peace is not statistically significant, and that the effect attributed to similarity is mostly driven by the pacifying effect of joint democracy.

Ray (2005) similarly disputes the weight of the argument on logical grounds, claiming that statistical analysis on "political similarity" uses a main variable which is an extension of "joint democracy" by linguistic redefinition, and so it is expected that the war reducing effects are carried on in the new analysis. Bennett (2006) builds a direct statistical model based on a triadic classification of states into "democratic", "autocratic" and "mixed".

He finds that autocratic dyads have a 35% reduced chance of going into any type of armed conflict with respect to a reference mixed dyad. Democratic dyads have a 55% reduced chance. This effect gets stronger when looking at more severe conflicts; for wars (more than 1000 battle deaths), he estimates democratic dyads to have an 82% lower risk than autocratic dyads. He concludes that autocratic peace exists, but democratic peace is clearly stronger. However, he finds no relevant pacifying effect of political similarity, except at the extremes of the scale.

To summarize a rather complex picture, there are no less than four possible stances on the value of this criticism:

1. Political similarity, plus some complementary variables, explains everything. Democratic peace is a statistical artifact. Henderson subscribes to this view.
2. Political similarity has a pacifying effect, but democracy makes it stronger. Werner would probably subscribe to this view.
3. Political similarity in general has little or no effect, except at the extremes of the democracy-autocracy scale: a democratic peace and an autocratic peace exist separately, with the first one being stronger,

and may have different explanations. Bennett holds this view, and Kinsella mentions this as a possibility

4. Political similarity has little or no effect and there is no evidence for autocratic peace. Petersen and Ray are among defendants of this view.

Economic Factors

A majority of researchers on the determinants of democracy agree that economic development is a primary factor which allows the formation of a stable and healthy democracy (Hegre, 2003; Weede, 2004). This in itself is not in contradiction with democratic peace theory; it is just a statement about the nature of democracy; however, if a causal link between some economic factor and peace could be found, one could hope to explain the findings of the theory on a purely economical basis.

Mousseau argues that a culture of contracting in advanced market-oriented economies may cause both democracy and peace (2000; 2002; 2003; 2005). These studies indicate that democracy, alone, is an unlikely cause of the democratic peace. A low level of market-oriented economic development may hinder development of liberal institutions and values. Hegre (2000) and Souva (2003) confirmed these expectations. Mousseau (2005) finds that democracy is a significant factor only when both democracies have levels of economic development well above the global median. In fact, the poorest 21% of the democracies studied, and the poorest 4-5% of current democracies, are significantly *more* likely than other kinds of countries to fight each other. Mousseau, Hegre & Oneal (2003) confirm that if at least one of the democracies involved has a very low level of economic development, democracy is ineffective in preventing war; however, they find that when also controlling for trade, 91% of all the democratic pairs had high enough development for the pacifying effect of democracy to be important during the 1885–1992 period and all in 1992. The difference in results of Mousseau (2005) and Mousseau, Hegre & Oneal (2003) may be due to sampling: Mousseau (2005) observed only neighboring states where poor countries actually can fight each other. In fact, fully 89% of militarized conflicts between less developed countries from 1920 and 2000 were among directly contiguous neighbors (Mousseau 2005:68-69). He argues that it is not likely that the results can be explained by trade: Because developed states have large economies, they do not have high levels of trade interdependence (2005:70 and footnote 5; Mousseau, Hegre & Oneal 2003:283). In fact, the correlation of developed democracy with trade interdependence is a scant 0.06 (Pearson's *r* - considered substantively no correlation by statisticians)(2005:77).

Both World Wars were fought between countries which can be considered economically developed. Mousseau argues that both Germany and Japan - like the USSR during the Cold War and Saudi Arabia today - had state-managed economies and thus lacked his market norms (Mousseau 2002-03:29). Hegre (2003) finds that democracy is correlated with civil peace only for developed countries, and for countries with high levels of literacy. Conversely, the risk of civil war decreases with development only for democratic countries.

Gartzke (2005) argues that economic freedom (a quite different concept from Mousseau's market norms) or financial dependence (2007) explains the developed democratic peace, and these countries may be weak on these dimensions too. Rummel (2005) criticizes Gartzke's methodology and argues that his results are invalid.

Several studies find that democracy, more trade causing greater economic interdependence, and membership in more intergovernmental organizations reduce the risk of war. This is often called the Kantian peace theory since it is similar to Kant's earlier theory about a perpetual peace; it is often also called "liberal peace" theory, especially when one focuses on the effects of trade and democracy. (The theory that free trade can cause peace is quite old and referred to as Cobdenism.)

Many researchers agree that these variables positively affect each other but each has a separate pacifying effect. For example, in countries exchanging a substantial amount of trade, economic interest groups may exist that oppose a reciprocal disruptive war, but in democracy such groups may have more power, and the political leaders be more likely to accept their requests. (Russett & Oneal 2001), (Lagazio & Russett 2004), (Oneal & Russett 2004). Weede (2004) argues that the pacifying effect of free trade and economic interdependence may be more important than that of democracy, because the former affects peace both directly and indirectly, by producing economic development and ultimately, democracy. Weede also lists some other authors supporting this view. However, some recent studies find no effect from trade but only from democracy (Goenner 2004), (Kim & Rousseau 2005).

None of the authors listed argues that free trade alone causes peace. Even so, the issue of whether free trade or democracy is more important in maintaining peace may have potentially significant practical consequences, for example on evaluating the effectiveness of applying economic sanctions and restrictions to autocratic countries.

Many studies, as those discussed in (Ray 1998), (Ray 2005), (Oneal & Russett 2004), supporting the theory have controlled for many possible alternative causes of the peace. Examples of factors controlled for are geographic distance, geographic contiguity, power status, alliance ties, militarization, economic wealth and economic growth, power ratio, and political stability. These studies have often found very different results depending on methodology and included variables, which has caused criticism. It should be noted that DPT does not state democracy is the only thing affecting the risk of military conflict.

Many of the mentioned studies have found that other factors are also important. However, a common thread in most results is an emphasis on the relationship between democracy and peace. Several studies have also controlled for the possibility of reverse causality from peace to democracy. For example, one study (Reuveny & Li 2003) supports the theory of simultaneous causation, finding that dyads involved in wars are likely to experience a decrease in joint democracy, which in turn increases the probability of further war. So they argue that disputes between democratizing or democratic states should be resolved externally at a very early stage, in order to stabilize the system. Another study (Reiter 2001) finds that peace does not spread democracy, but spreading democracy is likely to spread peace.

A different kind of reverse causation lies in the suggestion that impending war could destroy or decrease democracy, because the preparation for war might include political restrictions, which may be the cause for the findings of democratic peace. However, this hypothesis has been statistically tested in a study (Mousseau & Shi 1999) whose authors find, depending on the definition of the pre-war period, no such effect or a very slight one. So, they find this explanation unlikely. Note also that this explanation would predict a monadic effect, although weaker than the dyadic one.

Weart (1998) argues that the peacefulness appears and disappears rapidly when democracy appears and disappears. This in his view makes it unlikely that variables that change more slowly are the explanation. Weart, however, has been criticized for not offering any quantitative analysis supporting his claims (Ray, 2000). Wars tend very strongly to be between neighboring states. Gleditsch (1995) showed that the average distance between democracies is about 8000 miles, the same as the average distance between all states. He believes that the effect of distance in preventing war, modified by the democratic peace, explains the incidence of war as fully as it can be explained.

Realist View

Supporters of realism in international relations in general argue that not democracy or its absence, but considerations and evaluations of power, cause peace or war. Specifically, many realist critics claim that the effect ascribed to democratic, or liberal, peace, is in fact due to alliance ties between democratic states which in turn are caused, one way or another, by realist factors. For example, Farber and Gowa (1995) find evidence for peace between democracies to be statistically significant only in the period from 1945 on, and consider such peace an artifact of the Cold War, when the threat from the communist states forced democracies to ally with one another.

Mearsheimer (1990) offers a similar analysis of the Anglo-American peace before 1945, caused by the German threat. Spiro (1994) finds several instances of wars between democracies, arguing that evidence in favor of the theory might be not so vast as other authors report, and claims that the remaining evidence consists of peace between allied states with shared objectives. He acknowledges that democratic states might have a somewhat greater tendency to ally with one another, and regards this as the only real effect of democratic peace. Rosato (2003) argues that most of the significant evidence for democratic peace has been observed after World War II; and that it has happened within a broad alliance, which can be identified with NATO and its satellite nations, imposed and maintained by American dominance (see Pax Americana). One of the main points in Rosato's argument is that, although never engaged in open war with another liberal democracy during the Cold War, the United States intervened openly or covertly in the political affairs of democratic states several times, for example in the Chilean coup of 1973, the 1953 coup in Iran and 1954 coup in Guatemala; in Rosato's view, these interventions show the United States' determination to maintain an "imperial peace".

The most direct counter arguments to such criticisms have been studies finding peace between democracies to be significant even when controlling for "common interests" as reflected in alliance ties (Gelpi & Griesdorf 2001), (Ray 2003). Regarding specific issues, Ray (1998) objects that explanations based on the Cold War should predict that the Communist bloc would be at peace within itself also, but exceptions include the Soviet Invasion of Afghanistan, the Cambodian-Vietnamese War, and the Sino-Vietnamese War. Ray also argues that the external threat did not prevent conflicts in the Western bloc when at least one of the involved states was a nondemocracy, such as the Turkish Invasion of Cyprus (against Greek Junta supported Cypriot Greeks), the Falklands War, and the Football War. Also, one study (Ravlo & Gleditsch 2000) notes that the explanation "goes increasingly stale as the post-Cold War world accumulates an increasing number of peaceful dyad-years between democracies". Rosato's argument about American dominance has also been criticized for not giving supporting statistical evidence (Slantchev, Alexandrova & Gartzke 2005). Some realist authors also criticize in detail the explanations given by supporters of democratic peace, pointing to supposed inconsistencies or weaknesses.

Rosato (2003) criticizes most explanations to how democracy might cause peace. Arguments based on normative constraints, he argues, are not consistent with the fact that democracies do go to war no less than other states, thus violating norms preventing war; for the same reason he refutes arguments based on the importance of public opinion. Regarding explanations based on greater accountability of leaders, he finds that historically autocratic leaders have been removed or punished more often than democratic leaders when they get involved in costly wars. Finally, he also criticizes the arguments that democracies treat each other with trust and respect even during crises; and that democracy might be slow to mobilize its composite and diverse groups and opinions, hindering the start of a war, drawing support from other authors.

Another realist, Layne (1994) analyzes the crises and brinkmanship that took place between non-allied democratic great powers, during the relatively brief period when such existed. He finds no evidence either of institutional or cultural constraints against war; indeed, there was popular sentiment in favor of war on both sides. Instead, in all cases, one side concluded that it could not afford to risk that war at that time, and made the necessary concessions.

Rosato's objections have been criticized for claimed logical and methodological errors, and for being contradicted by existing statistical research (Slantchev, Alexandrova & Gartzke 2005), (Kinsella 2005). Russett (1995) replies to Layne by re-examining some of the crises studied in his article, and reaching different conclusions; Russett argues that perceptions of democracy prevented escalation, or played a major role in doing so.

Also, a recent study (Gelpi & Griesdorf 2001) finds that, while in general the outcome of international disputes is highly influenced by the contenders' relative military strength, this is not true if both contenders are democratic states; in this case the authors find the outcome of the crisis to be independent of the military capabilities of contenders, which is contrary to realist expectations. Finally, both the realist criticisms here described ignore new possible explanations, like the game-theoretic one discussed below. A different kind of realist criticism is centered around the role of nuclear weapons in maintaining peace. In realist terms, this means that, in the case of disputes between nuclear powers, respective evaluation of power might be irrelevant because of Mutual assured destruction preventing both sides from foreseeing what could be reasonably called a "victory". An obvious rebuttal is that nuclear powers have been too few to account for the evidence in favor of democratic peace, except a very small part of it. The rebuttal remains valid even considering the mitigating argument that some advanced democracies, for example Germany and Japan, would be able to complete a nuclear program in a very brief period of time if a possible nuclear menace arose. The 1999 Kargil War between India and Pakistan has been cited as a counterexample to this argument (Page Fortna, 2004).

Some supporters of the democratic peace do not deny that realist factors are also important (Russett 1995).

Research supporting the theory has also shown that factors such as alliance ties and major power status influence interstate conflict behavior (Ray 2003).

Marxist View

Immanuel Wallerstein has argued that it is the global capitalist system that creates shared interests among the dominant parties, thus inhibiting potentially harmful belligerence. Negri and Hardt take a similar stance, arguing that the intertwined network of interests in the global capitalism leads to the decline of individual nation states, and the rise of a global *Empire* which has no outside, and no external enemies. As a result, they write, "The era of imperialist, interimperialist, and anti-imperialist wars is over. (...) we have entered the era of minor and internal conflicts. Every imperial war is a civil war, a police action."

The peacefulness may have various limitations and qualifiers and may not actually mean very much in the real-world. Democratic peace researchers do in general not count as wars conflicts which do not kill a thousand on the battlefield; thus they exclude for example the bloodless Cod Wars. However, as noted earlier, research has also found a peacefulness between democracies when looking at lesser conflicts. Democracies were involved in more colonial and imperialistic wars than other states during the 1816-1945 period. On the other hand, this relation disappears if controlling for factors like power and number of colonies. Liberal democracies have less of these wars than other states after 1945.

This might be related to changes in the perception of non-European peoples, as embodied in the Universal Declaration of Human Rights (Ravlo & Glieditsch 2000). Related to this is the human rights violations committed against native people, sometimes by liberal democracies. One response is that many of the worst crimes were committed by nondemocracies, like in the European colonies before the nineteenth century, in King Leopold II of Belgium's privately owned Congo Free State, and in Stalin's Soviet Union. The United Kingdom abolished slavery in British territory in 1833, immediately after the Reform Act 1832 had significantly enlarged the franchise. (Of course, the abolition of the slave trade had been enacted in 1807; and many DPT supporters would deny that the UK was a liberal democracy in 1833 when examining interstate wars.)

Hermann and Kegley (1995) argue that interventions between democracies are more likely to happen than projected by an expected model. They further argue (1996) that democracies are more likely to intervene in other liberal states than against countries that are non-democracies. Finally, they argue that these interventions between democracies have been increasing over time and that the world can expect more of these interventions in the future. The methodology used has been criticized and more recent studies have found opposing results (Gleditsch, Christiansen & Hegre 2004).

Rummel argues that the continuing increase in democracy worldwide will soon lead to an end to wars and democide, possibly around or even before the middle of this century. The fall of Communism and the increase in the number of democratic states were accompanied by a sudden and dramatic decline in total warfare, interstate wars, ethnic wars, revolutionary wars, and the number of refugees and displaced persons. One report claims that the two main causes of this decline in warfare are the end of the Cold War itself and decolonization; but also claims that the three Kantian factors have contributed materially.

Importance

Democratic peace theory is a well established research field with more than a hundred authors having published articles about it. Several peer-reviewed studies mention in their introduction that most researchers accept the theory as an empirical fact. Imre Lakatos suggested that what he called a "progressive research program" is better than a "degenerative" one when it can explain the same phenomena as the "degenerative" one, but is also characterized by growth of its research field and the discovery of important novel facts. In contrast, the supporters of the "degenerative" program do not make important new empirical discoveries, but instead mostly apply adjustments to their theory in order to defend it from competitors.

Some researchers argue that democratic peace theory is now the "progressive" program in international relations. According to these authors, the theory can explain the empirical phenomena previously explained by the earlier dominant research program, realism in international relations; in addition, the initial statement that democracies do not, or rarely, wage war on one another, has been followed by a rapidly growing literature on novel empirical regularities. (Ray 2003), (Chernoff 2004), (Harrison 2005). Many of these derived studies have been mentioned above, for example those examining lesser conflicts and minor incidents.

Other examples are several studies finding that democracies are more likely to ally with one another than with other states, forming alliances which are likely to last longer than alliances involving nondemocracies (Ray 2003); several studies including (Weart 1998) showing that democracies conduct diplomacy differently and in a more conciliatory way compared to nondemocracies; one study finding that democracies with proportional representation are in general more peaceful regardless of the nature of the other party involved in a relationship (Leblang & Chan 2003); and another study reporting that proportional representation system and decentralized territorial autonomy is positively associated with lasting peace in postconflict societies (Binningsbø 2005).

Influence

The democratic peace theory has been extremely divisive among political scientists. It is rooted in the idealist and classical liberalist traditions and is opposed to the previously dominant theory of realism. However, democratic peace theory has come to be more widely accepted and has in some democracies effected policy change

Presidents of both the major United States parties have expressed support for the theory. Former President Bill Clinton of the Democratic Party: "Ultimately, the best strategy to ensure our security and to build a durable peace is to support the advance of democracy elsewhere. Democracies don't attack each other." Former President George W. Bush of the Republican Party: "And the reason why I'm so strong on democracy is democracies don't go to war with each other. And the reason why is the people of most societies don't like war, and they understand what war means.... I've got great faith in democracies to promote peace. And that's why I'm such a strong believer that the way forward in the Middle East, the broader Middle East, is to promote democracy."

Former European Commissioner for External Relations Chris Patten: "Inevitable because the EU was formed partly to protect liberal values, so it is hardly surprising that we should think it appropriate to speak out. But it is also sensible for strategic reasons. Free societies tend not to fight one another or to be bad neighbours." The *A Secure Europe in a Better World, European Security Strategy* states: "The best protection for our security is a world of well-governed democratic states." Tony Blair has claimed the theory is correct.

Some fear that the democratic peace theory may be used to justify wars against nondemocracies in order to bring lasting peace, in a *democratic crusade* (Chan 1997, p. 59). Woodrow Wilson in 1917 asked Congress to declare war against Imperial Germany, citing Germany's sinking of American ships due to unrestricted submarine warfare and the Zimmermann telegram, but also stating that "A steadfast concert for peace can never be maintained except by a partnership of democratic nations" and "The world must be made safe for democracy." R. J. Rummel is a notable proponent of war for the purpose of spreading democracy, based on this theory.

Some point out that the democratic peace theory has been used to justify the 2003 Iraq War, others argue that this justification was used only after the war had already started (Russett 2005). Furthermore, Weede (2004) has argued that the justification is extremely weak, because forcibly democratizing a country completely surrounded by non-democracies, most of which are full autocracies, as Iraq is, is at least as likely to increase the risk of war as it is to decrease it (some studies show that dyads formed by one democracy and one autocracy are the most warlike, and several find that the risk of war is greatly increased in democratizing countries surrounded by nondemocracies). According to Weede, if the United States and its allies wanted to adopt a rationale strategy of forced democratization based on democratic peace, which he still does not recommend, it would be best to start intervening in countries which border with at least one or two stable democracies, and expand gradually.

Also, research shows that attempts to create democracies by using external force has often failed. Gleditsch, Christiansen and Hegre (2004) argue that forced democratization by interventionism may initially have partial success, but often create an unstable democratizing country, which can have dangerous consequences in the long run. Those attempts which had a permanent and stable success, like democratization in occupied Japan after World War II, mostly involved countries which had an advanced economic and social structure already, and implied a drastic change of the whole political culture. Supporting internal democratic movements and using diplomacy may be far more successful and less costly.

7

Public Choice Theory

> "In politics we must choose between the strong man whose real interests are elsewhere and who will leave office the moment bigger opportunity beackons, and the weakling who will cling because he cannot hold a job anywhere else. Public office is the last refuge of the incompetent."
>
> —***Boise Penrose***

It is pertinent to note that Public choice in economic theory is the use of modern economic tools to study problems that are traditionally in the province of political science. From the perspective of political science, it may be seen as the subset of positive political theory which deals with subjects in which *material* interests are assumed to predominate.

More especially, it studies the behavior of politicians and government officials as mostly self-interested agents and their interactions in the social system either as such or under alternative constitutional rules. These can be represented a number of ways, including standard constrained utility maximization, game theory, or decision theory. Public choice analysis has roots in positive analysis ("what is") but is often used for normative purposes ("what ought to be"), to identify a problem or suggest how a system could be improved by changes in constitutional rules. Another related field is social choice theory.

It is remarkable that modern literature in Public Choice began with Duncan Black, who in 1948 identified the underlying concepts of what would become median voter theory. He also wrote *The Theory of Committees and Elections* in 1958. Gordon Tullock refers to him as the "father of public choice theory". James M. Buchanan and Gordon Tullock coauthored *The Calculus of Consent: Logical Foundations of Constitutional Democracy* (1962), considered one of the landmark works that founded the discipline of public choice theory. In particular (1962, p. v), the book is about the *political organization* of a free society. But its method, conceptual apparatus, and analytics "are derived, essentially, from the discipline that has as its subject the *economic* organization of such a society." The book focuses on positive-economic analysis as to the development of constitutional democracy but in an ethical context of consent.

The consent takes the form of a compensation principle like Pareto efficiency for making a policy change and unanimity at least no opposition as a point of departure for social choice. Kenneth Arrow's *Social Choice and Individual Values* (1951) influenced formulation of the theory. Among other important works are Anthony Downs's *An Economic Theory of Democracy* (1957) and Mancur Olson's *The Logic of Collective Action* (1965).

Public choice theory is commonly associated with George Mason University, where Tullock and Buchanan are currently faculty members. Their early work took place at the University of Virginia and Virginia Polytechnic Institute and State University, hence identification of a Virginia school of political economy. Development of public choice theory accelerated with the formation of the Public Choice Society in the United States in 1965. The loci of the Society became its journal *Public Choice* and its annual meetings.

The journal and meetings mainly attracted economists and political scientists. The economists brought their choice-based, model-building skill. The political scientists brought their broad knowledge of different political systems and detailed knowledge of institutions and political interaction. Scholars in related fields, such as philosophy, public administration, and sociology, also contributed.

Notably, in 1970 the median voter theory was accepted without question in public choice, but by 1980 it had been assaulted on so many fronts that it was almost abandoned. Works by Romer and Rosenthal (1979) and McKelvey (1976) showed that, when political issues are considered multidimensional rather than single dimensional, an agenda setter could start at any point in the issue space and, by strategically selecting issues, end up at any other point in the issue space, so that there is no unique and stable majority rule outcome. During the same decade, the probabilistic voting theory started to replace the median voter theory, since it clearly showed how it was able to find Nash Equilibria also in multidimensional space. The theory was later completely formalized by Peter Coughlin..

Special Interests

Public Choice theory is often used to explain how political decision-making results in outcomes that conflict with the preferences of the general public. For example, many advocacy group and pork barrel projects are not the desire of the overall democracy.

However, it makes sense for politicians to support these projects. It may make them feel powerful and important. It can also benefit them financially by opening the door to future wealth as lobbyists. The project may be of interest to the politician's local constituency, increasing district votes or campaign contributions. The politician pays little or no cost to gain these benefits, as he is spending public money. Special-interest lobbyists are also behaving rationally. They can gain government favors worth millions or billions for relatively small investments.

They face a risk of losing out to their competitors if they don't seek these favors. The taxpayer is also behaving rationally. The cost of defeating any one government give-away is very high, while the benefits to the individual taxpayer are very small. Each citizen pays only a few pennies or a few dollars for any given government favor, while the costs of ending that favor would be many times higher. Everyone involved has rational incentives to do exactly what they're doing, even though the desire of the general constituency is opposite.

Decision Making Processes and the State

One way to organize the subject matter studied by Public Choice theorists is to begin with the foundations of the state itself. According to this procedure, the most fundamental subject is the origin of government. Although some work has been done on anarchy, autocracy, revolution, and even war, the bulk of the study in this area has concerned the fundamental problem of collectively choosing constitutional rules. This work assumes a group of individuals who aim to form a government. Then it focuses on the problem of hiring the agents required to carry out government functions agreed upon by the members.

The main questions are: (1) how to hire competent and trustworthy individuals to whom day-to-day decision-making can be delegated and (2) how to set up an effective system of oversight and sanctions for such individuals. To answer these questions it is necessary to assess the effects of creating different loci of power and decision-making within a government; to examine voting and the various means of selecting candidates and choosing winners in elections; to assess various behavioral rules that might be established to influence the behavior of elected and appointed government officials; and to evaluate alternative constitutional and legal rights that could be reserved for citizens, especially rights relating to citizen oversight and the avoidance of harm due to the coercive power of government agents. These are difficult assessments to make. In practice, most work in the field of Public Choice has dealt with more limited issues. Extensive work has been done on different voting systems and, more generally, on how to transform what voters are assumed to want into a coherent "collective preference".

Of some interest has been the discovery that a general collective preference function cannot be derived from even seemingly mild conditions. This is often called Arrow's impossibility theorem. The theorem, an economic generalization of the voting paradox, suggests that voters have no reason to expect that, short of dictatorship, even the best rules for making collective decisions will lead to the kind of consistency attributed to individual choice. Much work has been done on the loose connection between decisions that we can imagine being made by a full contingent of citizens with zero collective decision-making costs and those made by legislators representing different voting constituencies.

Of special concern has been logrolling and other negotiations carried out by legislators in exercising their law-making powers. Important factors in such legislative decisions are political parties and pressure groups. Accordingly, Public Choicers have studied these institutions extensively.

The study of how legislatures make decisions and how various constitutional rules can constrain legislative decisions is a major sub-field in Public Choice.

Bureaucracy

Another major sub-field is the study of bureaucracy. The usual model depicts the top bureaucrats as being chosen by the chief executive and legislature, depending on whether the democratic system is presidential or parliamentary.

The typical image of a bureau chief is a person on a fixed salary who is concerned with pleasing those who appointed him. The latter have the power to hire and fire him more or less at will. The bulk of the bureaucrats, however, are civil servants whose jobs and pay are protected by a civil service system against major changes by their appointed bureau chiefs. This image is often compared with that of a business owner whose profit varies with the success of production and sales, who aims to maximize profit, and who can hire and fire employees at will.

Rent-Seeking

A field that is closely related to public choice is "rent-seeking." This field combines the study of a market economy with that of government. Thus, one might regard it as a "new political economy." Its basic thesis is that when both a market economy and government are present, government agents are a source of numerous special market privileges. Both the government agents and self-interested market participants seek these privileges in order to partake in the monopoly rent that they provide.

When such privileges are granted, they reduce the efficiency of the economic system. In addition, the rent-seekers use resources that could otherwise be used to produce goods that are valued by consumers. Rent-seeking is broader than Public Choice in that it applies to autocracies as well as democracies and, therefore, is not directly concerned with collective decision-making. However, the obvious pressures it exerts on legislators, executives, bureaucrats, and even judges are factors that Public Choicers must account for in their effort to understand and assess collective decision-making rules and institutions. Moreover, the members of a collective who are planning a government would be wise to take prospective rent-seeking into account.

Political Market Failure: Undemocratic Governments

Public Choice Theory has been developed largely in the context of democratic political systems of the variety that exist in Europe and North America. A pioneering work—and, perhaps, the only work to-date of its kind—seeking to analyze collective decision-making based on rules and institutions that characterize the Less Developed Countries was undertaken by Muzaffar Ali Isani at Georgetown University in 1982.

It focuses largely on the assumptions of a generation of development economists who have articulated the role of the state or political action as an efficient alternative to 'economic' market failures. Isani has suggested that once we introduce 'political' market imperfections as generally found in these countries, we may be confronted with the possibility that far from correcting market failures, political action may actually prove to be a source of further distortions in the economy. He then goes on to develop an essentially economic paradigm of politics appropriate to many developing countries and which is consistent with the axioms of economic theory.

Perspective

Prior to the emergence of public choice theory, many economists tended to consider the state as an agent outside the scope of economic theory, whose actions depend on different considerations than those driving economic agents.

Public choice theory attempts to look at governments from the perspective of the bureaucrats and politicians who compose them, and makes the assumption that they act based on Budget-maximizing model in a self-interested way for the purpose of maximizing their own economic benefits (e.g. their personal wealth). The theory aims to apply economic analysis (usually decision theory and game theory) to the political decision-making process in order to reveal certain systematic trends towards inefficient government policies. There are also Austrian variants of public choice theory (suggested by Mises, Hayek, Kirzner, Lopez, and Boettke) in which it is assumed that bureaucrats and politicians may be benevolent but have access to limited information. The assumption that such benevolent political agents possess limited information for making decisions often results in conclusions similar to those generated separately by means of the rational self-interest assumptions.

In another Austrian variant, developed by MacKenzie (2008a, 2008b), voters lack information on the opportunity costs of political choice, and expectation formation in politics is adaptive rather than rational. Randall Holcombe and Richard Wagner have also developed the notion of "Political Entrepreneurship".

One of the basic claims that results from public choice theory is that good government policies in a democracy are an underprovided public good, because of the rational ignorance of the voters. Each voter is faced with a tiny probability that his vote will change the result of the elections, while gathering the relevant information necessary for a well-informed voting decision requires substantial time and effort. Therefore, the rational decision for each voter is to be generally ignorant of politics and perhaps even abstain from voting. Rational choice theorists claim that this explains the gross ignorance of most citizens in modern democracies as well as low voter turnout. Rational abstention does, however, create the "Paradox of voting" whereby strict costs benefit analysis implies that nobody should vote.

Special Interests

While good government tends to be a pure public good for the mass of voters, there may be many advocacy groups that have strong incentives for lobbying the government to implement specific inefficient policies that would benefit them at the expense of the general public. For example, lobbying by the sugar manufacturers might result in an inefficient subsidy for the production of sugar, either direct or by protectionist measures. The costs of such inefficient policy are dispersed over all citizens, and therefore unnoticeable to each individual.

On the other hand, the benefits are shared by a small special-interest group with a strong incentive to perpetuate the policy by further lobbying. The vast majority of voters will be unaware of the effort due to rational ignorance. Therefore, theorists expect that numerous special interests will be able to successfully lobby for various inefficient policies. In public choice theory, such scenarios of inefficient government policies are referred to as *government failure* — a term akin to *market failure* from earlier theoretical welfare economics.

"Expressive Interests" and Democratic Irrationality

Geoffrey Brennan and Loren Lomasky claim that democratic policy is biased to favor "expressive interests" and neglect practical and utilitarian considerations. Brennan and Lomasky differentiate between instrumental interests (any kind of practical benefit, both monetary and non-monetary) and expressive interests (forms of expression like applause).

According to Brennan and Lomasky, the voting paradox can be resolved by differentiating between expressive and instrumental interests. While voters have virtually no instrumental incentive to vote, they do have an expressive interest in voting. Since voters vote for expressive reasons, politicians win by targeting the median expressive preferences. Bias in favor of expressive interests means that public policy often ignores important practical considerations.

For example, there are instrumental costs to restricting international trade. Yet many people favor protectionism as an expression of nationalism, despite its economic costs. This argument has led some public choice scholars to claim that politics is plagued by irrationality. In articles published in the Econ Journal Watch, economist Bryan Caplan contended that voter choices and government economic decisions are inherently irrational. Caplan's ideas are more fully developed in his book *The Myth of the Rational Voter* (Princeton University Press 2007).

In opposition to the arguments put forward by economist Donald Wittman in his The Myth of Democratic Failure, Caplan claims that politics is biased in favor of irrational beliefs. According to Caplan, democracy effectively subsidizes irrational beliefs. Anyone who derives utility from potentially irrational policies (such as protectionism) can receive private benefits while imposing the costs of such beliefs on the general public.

Were people to bear the full costs of their "irrational beliefs", they would lobby for them optimally, taking into account both their instrumental consequences and their expressive appeal. Instead, democracy oversupplies policies based on irrational beliefs. Caplan defines rationality mainly in terms of mainstream price theory, pointing out that mainstream economists tend to oppose protectionism and government regulation more than the general population, and that more educated people are closer to economists on this score, even after controlling for confounding factors such as income, wealth or political affiliation.

One criticism is that many economists do not share Caplan's views on the nature of public choice. However, Caplan does have some data to support his position. Economists have, in fact, often been frustrated by public opposition to economic reasoning. As Sam Peltzman puts it "Economists know what steps would improve the efficiency of HSE [health, safety, and environmental] regulation, and they have not been bashful advocates of them. These steps include substituting markets in property rights, such as emission rights, for command and control. . . . The real problem lies deeper than any lack of reform proposals or failure to press them.

Political Stance

From such results it is sometimes asserted that public choice theory has an anti-state tilt. But there is ideological diversity among public choice theorists. Mancur Olson for example was an advocate of a strong state and instead opposed political interest group lobbying. More generally,

James Buchanan has suggested that public choice theory be interpreted as "politics without romance," a critical approach to a pervasive earlier notion of idealized politics set against market failure. As such it is more a correction of the earlier scientific record, almost requiring a certain pragmatism in comparing alternative politicized institutional structures.

Remedies for the Public Choice Problem

Many proposals have been advanced for reducing what is often seen as excessive or improper influence on public choices by those who invest most to influence them. From game theory we have the insight that a winning strategy in competitive games should have a random component so that the opponent can't anticipate one's moves. This is confirmed by the historical resort to having decisions made by officials selected at random, perhaps with a complex process of intermediate qualifying steps, called sortition. That is what is done in countries using a trial jury selected at random.

Applications

Public choice's application to government regulation was developed by George Stigler (1971) and Sam Peltzman (1976). William Niskanen is generally considered the founder of Public Choice literature on the bureaucracy.

It is remarkable that notable Public Choice scholars have been awarded the Nobel Prize in Economics, including James M. Buchanan (1986), George Stigler (1982), and Gary Becker (1992). In addition, Vernon Smith (2002) was President of Public Choice Society from 1988 to 1990.

A Critical Analysis

In their 1994 book *Pathologies of Rational Choice Theory*,

political scientists Donald P. Green and Ian Shapiro argue that rational choice theory (of which public choice theory is a branch) has contributed less to the field than its popularity suggests. They write:

> The discrepancy between the faith that practitioners place in rational choice theory and its failure to deliver empirically warrants closer inspection of rational choice theorizing as a scientific enterprise.

Linda McQuaig writes in *All You Can Eat*:

> The absurdity of public-choice theory is captured by Nobel Prize-winning economist Amartya Sen in the following little scenario: "Can you direct me to the railway station?" asks the stranger. "Certainly," says the local, pointing in the opposite direction, towards the post office, "and would you post this letter for me on your way?" "Certainly," says the stranger, resolving to open it to see if it contains anything worth stealing.

It should be noted that scenarios of this type contain an implicit assumption of zero probability of the two strangers ever interacting again. With a positive probability of future interactions and the propensity of humans to use tit-for-tat type strategies (someone harms or helps you, you return the favor in kind), the optimal totally self-interested decision may be to point to the train station.

Furthermore, as David D. Friedman observes, the benefit of cheating the stranger *on one occasion* may not be worth the mental effort of conceiving a way to do so and weighing the odds of suffering the consequences.

Public Choice theorists have been criticized for failure to explain human actions motivated by non-rational or non-economic considerations. They respond, however, that the theory explains a broad variety of actions since humanitarian or even a madman's actions are also rational. This way, the argument goes, public choice allows to account for a much broader variety of actions than any other approach, and in the example above, Sen's rational actors may or may not act in a way he identified, since public choice approach does not mean the actors necessarily take advantage of one another; it only implies that the actions are 'rational'.

Action to direct someone to a train station would thus be just as rational as the action to direct the stranger away for one's own reasons. Furthermore, only 'rationalism' helps to explain human motivation, whereas any other approaches such as humanitarian considerations or the willingness to get extra profit (which is in no way the same as 'rational action') would only explain a part of the developments and fails to present a comprehensive picture. Also, Bryan Caplan argues against rationality in politics, and Brennan and Lomasky account for expressive (non-economic) motives in politics. Schram and Caterino (2006) contains a fundamental methodological criticism of public choice theory for promoting the view that the natural science model is the only appropriate methodology in social science and that political science should follow this model, with its emphasis on quantification and mathematization. Schram and Caterino argue instead for methodological pluralism.

8

Political Methodology

Over the past four decades political methodology has meant primarily applications and extensions of whatever econometricians were using. The main theme of this chapter is that the importation of econometric methods has substantially advanced the practice of empirical work in political science and provided very important substantive insights. This progress, and it definitely is progress, has come with an opportunity cost. The economists' sermon of no free lunch applies in the application of econometrics as well. The cost is in the form of assumptions that are widely accepted in economics and deeply imbedded in their statistical models.

The application and refinement of econometric techniques has been the dominant theme of political methodology for the past twenty-five years. The expansion of these techniques is well documented by King (1991) and the impressive array of applications to substantive as well as methodological questions is thoroughly covered by Bartels and Brady (1993). It is easy to see the reasons for the rapid and extensive spread of these techniques. As developed by economists for studying economic behaviour and testing economic theories, they are much better suited to the non-experimental nature of most political science research than the quasi-experimental techniques, such as cross-tabulation, analysis of variance, and tests of association, commonly used by earlier political methodologists.

Econometric techniques, as exemplified by but not limited to the least-squares estimator, focus attention on the model of the behaviour being investigated and not just on the association among a small set of variables of interest. This attention to model specification has now gone well beyond a concern for which variables belong in the analysis to include such questions as functional form, endogeneity, and measurement. All of these questions are central to the analysis of political phenomena. The linear estimation model is very powerful in two ways that go beyond its statistical properties. First, the model itself is quite robust in the face of a wide array of difficulties.

It often takes extreme deviations from the basic assumptions to produce highly suspicious results. In some instances, even with violations of its basic assumptions the generalised version of the linear model provides estimates with a smaller mean squared error than more theoretically correct, but less robust, estimators (Beck and Katz 1995).

The second and far more important form of robustness, call it adaptability, is the ability of an army of methodologists to apply and extend the basic methodological strategy to widely varied situations. Most work of political methodologists in the past twenty-five years has been a successful effort to extend the basic model to an ever broader set of problems and to overcome an increasingly wide set of violations of the basic model.

As Bartels and Brady (1993) demonstrate in thirty pages of text and nearly eight-and-a-half pages of citations this has been a successful endeavor in political science. After reading the Bartels and Brady chapter, it is fair to say that work with this basic model has led to significant findings and new ways of thinking in virtually all areas of the discipline. Where once empirical methods may have been largely the province of Americanists, or even more accurately Americanists doing political behaviour, methodologists are found in most subfields, and the econometric approach, in its many variations, provides the unifying language.

Three different applications—structural equation models, time-series analysis, and non-linear estimation—will illustrate this adaptability -to sophisticated conceptual models and to a wide range of problems arising from the non-experimental nature of social science research. The rest if this section provides a quick summary of these three adaptations.

Structural equation estimation treats entire sets of variables as jointly determined and stochastic. Applications derived from statistics develops; for experimental situations assume that all explanatory variables are see outside the experiment and can be considered fixed and non-stochastic, This is a dubious assumption for the non-experimental setting where many of the variables of interest interact and cannot be treated as pre-determined or exogenous even though they appear as explanatory variables in some parts of the model. Econometricians discussed this problem extensively and provided a variety of approaches, such as instrumental variables, two and three stage least-squares and *k*-class estimators (Judge *et al.* 1985 offer good coverage of these methods). These methods have many application in political science, where the examination of the asymmetric, or simultaneous, relationships among endogenous variables is central to testing important theoretical propositions. They have been used to examine party identification, vote decisions, the connection between economic conditions and votes, and the influence of Senate leaders.

A major use of structural equation models is to incorporate systematic hypotheses about measurement error and missing variables into a wide variety of models. A major reason why the explanatory variables in an otherwise straightforward regression model are stochastic is the presence of random measurement errors. The consequence of these errors is to bias all efficient estimates, with the direction and amount of bias dependent upon the covariances among the true and the included variables (Achen 1985). Joreskog (1973) and Joreskog and Sorbom (1979) showed that the general form of the structural equation model incorporated both random measurement error and simultaneity as special cases. This general model, properly referred to as the multiple indicator multiple cause (or MIMC), model also permitted estimation of sophisticated model with latent, or missing variables. One of the most significant extensions of the work with missing variables was Franklin's development of a procedure for simulating the analysis of panel data from successive cross-sections (Franklin 1990). Applications with both measurement error and latent variables are seen in most subfields, though the most extensive use has been in the analysis of survey data.

Time-series Analysis

The second area of major innovation is the analysis of time-series data. Many of the important conceptual arguments and substantive interests concern how behaviour, institutions, and outcomes vary over time and in response to specific interventions and shocks. Concerns as varied as determinants of presidential approval (Beck 1992), arms races (Williams and McGinnis 1988; McGinnis and Williams 1989), the political business cycle (Beck 1987), partisanship (MacKuen, Erikson and Stimson 1989; Smith and Box-Steffensmeier 1995), and government expenditures in Britain are addressed with time-series data.

Rigorous examination of time-series data began with the use of simple autoregressive integrated moving average (ARIMA) models to study the over time fluctuations of individual variables (see Hibbs (1974) for the introduction of these techniques to political science). Much of this work suffered from an absence of a priori theorising and a lack of attention to covariation among variables leading to very weak causal inferences.

This work, however, has now been extended to include very sophisticated multi-variate analyses of systems of variables which has substantially strengthened the resulting inferences. Strong attention is now paid to the existence of multi-period lags and to the patterns of covariations among the lags of sets of variables. In methods such as Vector Autoregression (VAR) strong inferences about exogeneity and the reaction of the system to external shocks are derived from these covariations (see Freeman, Williams and Lin 1989; Williams and McGinnis 1988; McGinnis and Williams 1989).

Some of the most sophisticated time-series analyses, referred to as cointegration and error correction models, begin with the assumption of a system of variables with a long-term equilibrium. Data are then analysed to estimate the characteristics of this equilibrium, how the system responds to shocks that move it out of equilibrium, and the time required for the effects of the shock to dissipate.

These are only a small portion of the extension and application developed over recent years. They do, however, give a clear indication of the range and significance of the models and problems that have been examined through adaptations of the basic estimation model. It is this adaptability and generalisability of the econometric model and its appro-priateness for non-experimentally generated data that have made the model so dominant.

King (1989a) with only a small amount of exaggeration, can legitimately talk about unifying political methodology under the banner of the more general form of the estimation model imported from statistics through economics. As in virtually all intellectual endeavors, this progress in the development and expansion of methodological techniques and in their application to an increasingly broad set of issues is predicated on certain assumptions.

We are frequently reminded, sometimes after the fact, of some of these assumptions, such as having iid disturbances, some known distribution for the observed or unobserved variables, a priori belief in the exogeneity of certain variables; the appropriateness of some linear or non-linear form, etc. There is one assumption that is basic, but less frequently questioned, to all the current estimation models. This is the idea that a predictable stable equilibrium underlies the process being studied and generating the observed data. Stochastic terms are treated as deviations about this assumed equilibrium.

These deviations may be biased in certain cases or acquire particularly noxious characteristics in others, but fundamentally the techniques are premised on the existence of this equilibrium so that appropriate techniques can then be developed to deal with the pathological deviations.

Then with enough observations one can obtain reliable estimates of the parameters in this system. The remainder of this chapter explores the "What if" question posed by models of processes that may not fit this equilibrium assumption.

Alternative Approach

The equilibrium centered model and the comparative statics analyses that are derived from it have enabled social scientists to describe and understand a wide range of important phenomena. But there are also processes and institutions that are poorly described in this manner. The motivation for this chapter is an increasing interest in these processes and institutions. The discussion of alternatives will focus on the class of behaviours that are frequently referred to as "path dependent." A path dependent process may well reach a stable equilibrium at some point, but the characteristics of that equilibrium are partially a function of the sequence of actions or intermediate outcomes obtained as part of the equilibrating process. The initial and exogenous factors alone are insufficient for predicting the equilibrium-One way to put this is that, "Where you end up depends upon how you got there."

Probably the simplest version of a path-dependent model is the urn problem described by Arthur and his statistical colleagues (Arthur *et al* 1987). In this problem, one starts with an urn with one red and one white ball (could statisticians start any other way?). A ball is withdrawn, and it and a second ball of the same color are placed back in this urn. This process is repeated an infinite number of times. The process finally reaches a stable point where the proportion of red and white balls remains constant (probability limits are useful).

The fundamental point of the model is that there are multiple equilibria and that the one ultimately reached is strongly related to the sequence of balls selected in the early trials. For example, drawing a red ball on the first two trials makes an equilibrium with a majority of white balls much less likely than if white balls were drawn in these trials. The urn problem becomes a nice metaphor for many path dependent type political and social processes.

A. Public Preferences, Political Institutions, and Path Dependence

The two most significant explicit demonstrations of path-dependent processes in political science examine the connections between mass public issue preferences and the performance of U.S. political institutions. The first, and most ambitious, is Carmines and Stimson's study of the connection between the actions of the Congress on civil rights legislation and the evolution of public opinion (Carmines and Stimson 1989). They use tune-series data to show that changes in the positions taken by Republicans and Democrats in the House and the Senate on Civil Rights legislation during the late 1950s and early 1960s led changes in public opinion on that issue. They conclude that these party shifts led to a substantial evolution in the structure and alignment of the parties.

The model posits that the mass issue evolution begins with a "critical moment"—more visible than the creepingly slow change implied by pure secular realignment but much less pronounced than that presumed by critical election realignments. Equally significant, the initial increase in mass issue polarisation does not complete the process but only begins it by setting in motion a change that grows over time. Dynamic evolutions thus represent the political equivalent of biology's punctuated equilibrium. The critical moment corresponds to the punctuation point—a change of some magnitude but not a cataclysmic adaptation. The slower, continuous change following the critical moment is the drive toward a new equilibrium—the semipermanent redefinition of the link between issues and mass parties.

They do not pursue what the new equilibrium might be or how it relates to the initial conditions and to the punctuation point, or shock, that disturbed the existing equilibrium; A fair surmise is that the link between issues and mass parties referred to is a complex one, as it must include a connection from mass opinion to the behaviour of the parties and of Congress.

The exact nature of these mutual relationships will determine the path from one equilibrium to the next. The analytical expressions for such a link, and the effort required to test propositions about the expected equilibrium, will be very daunting for a system as complex as one involving mass preferences, parties, and a two chamber legislature.

Remarkably, second study to propose a path-dependent type process is the study of endogenous preferences by Gerber and Jackson (1993). They also examine the link between elite behaviour and mass preferences, but in the context of a model of electoral competition. They argue from a series of cross-sectional analyses of survey data on civil rights and Vietnam opinions that shifts in party positions provide information that induces voters to alter their preferences. They speculate that placing endogenous preferences in a full model of electoral competition will create an electoral system that resembles a path-dependent dynamic process. Gerber and Jackson concluded that,

> Endogenous preferences introduce a dynamic element into the traditional static electoral model.... Specifically outcomes

> become less predictable. An equilibrium may exist under a variety of initial conditions, but any result will be partially dependent upon the sequence and timing of party platforms and upon how rapidly the parties change positions (652-3).

Notably, Jackson (1994) then pursues this speculation more formally. He shows both analytically and through simulation that a simple one-dimensional model of two-party competition with endogenous preferences has an equilibrium, denned as a stable set of preferences and party positions. The characteristics of this equilibrium, however, depend upon the sequence of party positions following any shock that disrupts the previous equilibrium—a path-dependent process. These two studies raise interesting and provocative speculations about the course of U.S. political history over the past forty years—a very path-dependent process. The Carmines and Stimson and Gerber and Jackson studies describe the startling shifts in party positions and leadership behaviour on the civil rights issue during the 1950s and 1960s.

The dramatic differences between Goldwater's and Johnson's positions on the Civil Rights Act of 1964, and with their party's previous positions, produced a radical shift in the voting patterns in that election. These strategies and shifts led eventually, but directly, to a realignment of the electorate and of the regional allocation of Congressional seats. Consider whether we would have a Newt Gingrich or have had a Democratic Senate Leader from Maine without this historical event.

B. Path Dependency and Models of Political Economy

This concept of evolution and path dependence is becoming central to the discussions and study of many other political and economic processes and institutions, with very important implications and consequences. North (1990), for example, devotes a considerable amount of attention in his book on institutions and economic performance to a discussion of the importance of path dependence. He contends, but does not illustrate empirically, that the design of economic and political institutions is central to the development process and that transactions costs, interacting with the particular institutions in place, create a strongly path-dependent process.

Riker and Weimer (1993), while citing North, take the argument even further in their discussion of the importance of property rights in the former Socialist countries. They are particularly concerned about institutional design in these societies and argue that the creation of economic and political institutions begins a path-dependent process, without resorting to discussions of transaction costs. Arguments for the presence and significance of path-dependent processes can rest on more than institutional questions and extend outside political science. Krugman's (1991) description of regional economic development includes the importance of agglomeration, or economy of scale effects, which makes the model explicitly path dependent. (This work has significance beyond the regional economic field, as it applies to differences in the growth rates of countries, and thus to international political economy as well.)

His model of growth incorporates the main features of Arthur *et al.'s* urn problem and explains the geographic concentration of various industries, such as automobiles in southeast Michigan, semiconductors in northern California, etc.

Here our concern is that given the central interests of political scientists in the performance and evolution of economic and political institutions, models that incorporate path dependency in some form will and should become an important part of our formal theories. The question for political methodologists is how well do the empirical methods, largely imported from econometrics, perform in identifying path-dependent processes, in estimating the form and parameters in these processes, and in testing important hypotheses. Our intuition is that because these econometric methods are built on the assumption of a static and exogenously determined equilibrium, they may not perform as well as desired or as needed. The remainder of the chapter tries to shed some light on this question through various analytical and simulation exercises.

Path-dependent Example

It is possible, and useful, to illustrate the results obtained using the standard econometric techniques by applying them to simulated data sets where the underlying process generating the data is known. In the applications developed here, one data set will represent a system with an equilibrium determined solely by the predetermined variables and any exogenous shocks. Other data sets will be collected from a system with an equilibrium, but where this equilibrium is a result of the path taken as the system moves from one equilibrium to another in response to exogenous shocks. To further illustrate the hazards and consequences of analysing path-dependent systems with conventional tools, these data will be generated with alternative models and with different sequences of shocks to show the different equilibria, and the different econometric results. This section first describes the model, in both its static and dynamic equilibrium forms. We then discuss the simulated data sets generated with each version of the model, and compare the results of a statistical analysis of each data set.

A. A Dynamic Model of Two-party Competition

The data used to illustrate what standard econometric techniques reveal about different classes of models are generated by a simulation model of two-party electoral competition over a single dimension. This model is selected because of its known equilibrium properties and its centrality in the formal political theory literature.

The significant variation is that in one version the distribution of individuals' preferences shifts as the parties change their positions, making this distribution endogenous to the political process. In the traditional model, our baseline, preferences are fixed and can be used to predict the equilibrium outcome. In the general model there is an equilibrium outcome, but it cannot be predicted from the initial or exogenous conditions because the location of the equilibrium depends upon the sequence of positions taken by the competing parties as they seek this new equilibrium.

The essence of the model is very simple. In the traditional, and simplest, 'model of two-party competition the utility, or loss, each voter associates with a party's position is represented as a quadratic function of the distance between the person's preferred policy and that advocated by the party. The voter is then assumed to vote for the closest party, defined as the one associated with the least loss, or greatest utility. Citisens develop a partisanship based on a similar utility calculation, though partisanship is presumed to have a longer lag and to be more likely to include past issue-based utility calculations. (For a theoretical argument about the evolution of partisanship, see Achen (1992). Jackson (1975&) and Franklin and Jackson (1983) provide empirical results supporting this formal model.) In this version of the model, it is assumed that each voter's preferred policy remains fixed during the period in which the parties are choosing, or searching for, their optimal platforms. Under these simple conditions, the median of the distribution of voters' preferences becomes the equilibrium. (If the preference distribution is symmetric, or if there is probabilistic voting, then the mean becomes the equilibrium outcome.) If parties only want to maximise their likelihood of election, then each party eventually adopts the preference median, or mean, as its strategy.

If parties place an intrinsic value on their platform, as well as on getting elected, an equilibrium still exists, but with the parties a fixed distance from the median, depending upon how strongly they value their platform relative to their proportion of the votes. A main feature of this model is that if there is a sudden shift in, or shock to, the distribution of individual preferences, the system would reach a new equilibrium. More significantly, the main features of this equilibrium—the means of the distributions of issue preferences, partisanship, and vote eval-uations and the positions of the two parties—are predictable from the size and direction of the exogenously given shock. The path, or sequence of positions, the parties take in reaching this new equilibrium will be irrele-vant Similarly, if there were a series of shocks following periods of equilib-rium, we would predict the final state simply by knowing the initial conditions and the value of each shock.

Incorporating the evolutionary model of issue-preference evolution proposed by Carmines and Stimson (1989) and by Gerber and Jackson (1993) substantially alters this version of the electoral model. In the evolutionary version, the actions and choice of the various political actors and parties exert an influence on citizens' preference. This change can be accommodated with an additional equation in the voting model. This addition is a Bayesian expression, where individuals update their issue preferences based on changes in the parties' positions. The argument here is that individuals have some uncertainty about their policy preferences and party positions provide cues to partisans about how much they might like various policies. Changes in party positions provide new information which leads these partisans to update their preferences.

If the policy preferences and partisanship of individual i at time t are denoted by X_{it} and P_{it} respectively and the two parties and their positions by θ_t and ϕ_t, the model of preference updating is,

$$\overline{X}_t = Z_t + B_{1t}X_{it-1} + (1 - B_{1t})[.5B_2(\theta_t - \phi_t)P_{it}],$$

were $B_{1t} = e^{-B_1(\Delta\theta_t^2 + \Delta\phi_t^2)}$. (Stochastic terms are omitted from all subsequent equations in order to concentrate the discussion and comparisons on the systematic parts of the different models and analyses.) The variable Z_t represents any exogenously generated shift in mean preferences that would upset an existing equilibrium. This expression is linear in the individual variables, so that dropping the i subscripts gives the following expression for the mean of the preference distribution at time t, $\overline{X}_t$:

$$\overline{X}_t = Z_t + B_{1t}X_{it-1} + (1 - B_{1t})[.5B_2(\theta_t - \phi_t)P_{it}],$$

The model used in the rest of the chapter concentrates on expressions for the aggregate electoral properties.

In this formulation, $[B_2(\theta_t - \phi_t)P_{it}]$ is the informational cue, and the amount of change in party positions from t–1 to t, $(\Delta\theta_t^2 + \Delta\phi_t^2)$, indicates the relative variance, or certainty, of the new information. No change in party positions indicates no new information and B_{1t}= 1 and preferences remain unchanged. As the amount of change in party positions increases, the weight given to the informational cue increases and the weight given to previous preferences decreases, assuming $B_1 > 0$. If $B_1 = 0$ then $B_{1t} = 1$ regardless of any change in party positions, which makes the previous model with exogenously determined preferences a special case of the current model.

The rest of the model contains expressions for mean partisanship, $\overline{P}$ mean vote evaluations, $\overline{V}$, and the positions of the two competing parties, θ and ϕ. Individual partisanship and vote evaluations follow the traditional quadratic utility model, which also gives simple aggregate expressions,

$$\overline{P}_t = (1 - B_3)\overline{P}_{t-1} + 2_\alpha B_3 D_r \overline{X}_t -_\alpha B_3(\theta_t^2 - \phi_t^2),$$

$$V_t = (1 + B_4)\overline{P}_t + 2_\alpha B_4 D_r \overline{X}_t -_\alpha B_4(\theta_t^2 - \phi_t^2).$$

The equilibrium values for $\overline{P}$ and $\overline{V}$ are identical and are,

$$\overline{P}^* = \overline{V}^* = 2_\alpha(\theta^* - \phi^*)\overline{X}^* - \alpha(\theta^{*2} - \phi^{*2}).$$

Parties value their probability of winning election, the log-odds of which is linearly related to $\overline{V}$, and their platform. The desired platforms are fixed and denoted by $G\theta = G$ and $G_\phi = -G$. The parties' utility functions are quite arbitrarily selected and contain a single parameter γ that measures the importance of the desired platform relative to the probability of winning. For a given $\overline{X}$ and $\overline{V}$ *the* utility-maximising platforms are,

$$\theta^* = \frac{_\alpha(B_3 + B_4 - B_3B_4)(1-\gamma)\overline{X} + \gamma G(1 + e^{\overline{V}})}{_\alpha(B_3 + B_4 - B_3B_4)(1-\gamma) + \gamma G(1 + e^{\overline{V}})}$$

$$\phi^* = \frac{_\alpha(B_3 + B_4 - B_3B_4)(1-\gamma)\overline{X} + \gamma G(1+e^{\overline{V}})}{_\alpha(B_3 + B_4 - B_3B_4)(1-\gamma) + \gamma G(1+e^{\overline{V}})}$$

Parties are assumed to adjust their platform towards the utility-maximising position, if they are not already there. The adjustment parameter is denoted by δ, so that

$$\theta_{t+1} = (1-\delta)\theta_t + \delta\theta_t^* \text{ and}$$

$$\theta_{t+1} = (1-\delta)\theta t + \delta\theta_t^*$$

The model with endogenous preferences, $B_1 > 0$, is important because the distribution of preferences is likely to shift with changes in party positions. The new equilibrium after a shift in preferences, i.e. a $Z_t = \neq 0$, cannot be predicted by knowing only $\overline{X}_{t-1}$ and Z_t as would be the case with fixed preferences, $B_1 = 0$.

B. Simulations of Electoral Competition

The model of electoral competition Just outlined was developed as a simulation model that can produce a series of elections and generate time-series data describing the outcomes of these elections, θ_t, ϕ_t, and $\overline{V}_t$ and $\overline{V}_t$ respectively. The basic parameters are chosen arbitrarily, with $\alpha = .5$, $B_1 = 0$ or 1, $B_2 = 1.25$, $B_3 = .5$, $B_4 = .5$, $\gamma = 1/3$, and $G = 2$ for all replications. These elections can be conducted following different scenarious, denned as different values for δ and different sequences of shocks, Z_t, and the data from each analysed with various statistical methods. Comparisons of the statistical results permit evaluations of how well these methods help us understand the different processes. The prediction is that the methods will do very well at reproducing the system with exogenous preferences and much less well for the path-dependent processes.

The basic structure of the simulations is the same in all replications. The model is started at equilibrium, with the mean preference equal to zero and the two parties located at ±1.4545, respectively. Every twenty-eighth iteration a random number is drawn from a standard uniform distribution with mean zero and assigned to $\in_t$. With each shock, mean preferences are assumed to follow an ARMA(1,1) process where $\overline{X}_t = .9\overline{X}_{t-1} + Z_t$ and $Z_t = \in_t - .8_{\in t-1}$ (The parameter values for this equation are chosen arbitrarily, but are done so as to conform closely to eqn. 8 and to generate a stationary series for $\overline{X}_t$ with a variance close to that of the stochastic term $\in_t$) This simulates the effect of a random shock to preferences that upsets the existing equilibrium. The interval of twenty-eight periods between shocks is chosen solely to insure that the system reaches equilibrium.

After the twenty-eighth interval, and just prior to the next shock, the values of the variables in the model are recorded as measures of the electoral outcomes. First-order conditions were computed at each iteration and printed along with the other output. These were always less than $.5 \times 10^{-6}$, indicating that an equilibrium had been reached. (Other analyses were done to assure that these were stable equilibria.) This sequence of an exogenous shock followed by periods for equilibration is repeated 100 times, giving an electoral time series of 100 observations, excluding the t_0 period. These observations become the data for the different estimation methods.

The most important comparisons of the statistical results are not between the static simulation and the two simulations with endogenous preferences but between the two simulations with endogenous preferences and between the corresponding replications in each scenario. Differences in the results from analysing the two scenarios indicate the sensitivity of the methods to the path dependency of the different equilibria created by the parties adopting different strategies. Differences across replications of the same scenario demonstrate any sensitivity of the statistical results to variations in the exogenously determined histories. This is an equally disturbing result if the variations are very large, since the statistical analysis incorporates the information from each history.

C. Reduced Form Estimation

The first estimations are reduced form models relating the equilibrium outcomes to the predetermined and exogenous variables, Ay-i and *Zi* respectively. In the scenario with the static equilibrium model these estimations should give an accurate picture of the true model as there are no stochastic terms. For the other two scenarios, it is less obvious what to expect, though intuition suggests that results may differ, both from the static model and between the two scenarios because the equilibrium outcomes are not strictly related to the predetermined conditions.

The equations replicate the true model and there is virtually no variation in the estimated coefficients for the twenty replications. The fits are not shown, but the R^2 are 1.000 for the preference, partisanship and vote equations and above 0.998 for the party position equations. These results mean that knowing the starting condi-tions and the sequence of shocks allows one to reproduce the system. When the underlying model perfectly fits the assumptions of the statistical model—that the equilibrium is perfectly predictable from the predeter-mined conditions—the statistical methods perform very well.

As expected, the statistical results do not reproduce the true model and they exhibit considerable variation across replications. These differences and variations are particularly large for the scenario with very adaptive parties, $\delta = .8$. Two concerns evolve from these results. One is that variations in party strategies, which create different histories of an endogenous sort, produce different equilibria, as attested to by the fact that the correlation between the equilibrium mean preference for these two scenarios is only 0.58, even though their starling-points and sequences of exogenous shocks are identical.

These different equilibria, in turn, give very different statistical results, even when averaged over twenty replications. The second concern is that even within a given scenario, where the true models are exactly identical and all the exogenous information is included in the statistical analysis, different sequences of shocks produce different results. The standard deviations and the ranges of the estimated co-efficients across the twenty replications with $\delta = .80$ indicate the sensitivity particularly well. The scenario with $\delta = .65$ exhibits substantially less sensitivity, but this scenario is designed to have less party movement, and therefore to exhibit less path dependency.

D. Structural Equation Estimation

The second econometric comparison estimates the structural equations of the model using these data. Again, we know the true model, so specification uncertainty is not an issue. Structural estimation is a much more demanding, but also more significant, exercise as these estimations should provide evidence about the underlying structure of the process and about what factors are endogenous and which are exogenous.

Estimation of these equations presents several statistical' challenges, and demonstrates the econometric tools discussed earlier. This is a nonrecursive structural equation system with jointly determined endogenous variables. If there were stochastic terms, as one confronts with real data, this would necessitate the use of an instrumental variables or comparable estimator to purge the explanatory variables of their confounding effects.

There are no stochastic terms here, but we will use an instrumental variables procedure nonetheless. All contemporaneous variables are treated as endogenous, with the lagged values of each variable and the shock, Z_t, used as predetermined variables to create instruments. Instruments will be created directly for the nonlinear variables, such as $(\theta_t - \phi_t.)\overline{X}_t$. With these transformations, the equations for partisanship, vote evaluations and preferences can be estimated directly as they are linear in the parameters.

Estimation of the equations for party positions recover the true model for the scenario with exogenous preferences, with no variation across replications. This is what is expected. What is notable is that this estimation uses a nonlinear least-squares method, illustrating the adaptability noted earlier. This method does reasonably well with the scenarios with endogenous preferences, though there is a clear downward bias to the estimates of the party utility for their own platform, γ, and an upward bias to the estimate of the desired platform, *G*. Only for the scenario with $\delta =$ .80 do these biases and variations across replications become particularly noticeable.

The most startling contrasts are the estimated equations for $\overline{X}_t$. As expected, with exogenous preferences, the equation is estimated perfectly. For the two scenarios with endogenous preferences, however, there are completely contradictory results. The mean of the replications for δ = .65 implies that $\overline{X}$ is strictly an endogenous variable that is not affected by either its lagged value or the exogenous shock. The replications with δ = .80 imply just the opposite, with the mean coefficient on the endogenous term being close to zero and the mean coefficients on the lagged and shock terms being large and positive. The coefficients on $\overline{X}_{t-1}$ and Z_t have large variation over the replications for each scenario, indicating that even for the same value of δ there are results with very different implications. The estimated equations for the first replication for each value of δ and for the eighth replication for δ = .65 exhibit these two different, but troubling contrasts.

$$\overline{X}_t = -.21 + .97\overline{X}_{t-1} + 1.26Z_t - .04(\theta_t - \phi_t)\overline{P}_t \quad \delta = .80, \text{Rep} = 1$$

$$\overline{X}_t = .00 + .00\overline{X}_{t-1} + .01Z_t + .26(\theta_t - \phi_t)\overline{P}_t \quad \delta = .65, \text{Rep} = 1$$

$$\overline{X}_t = -.18 + .83\overline{X}_{t-1} + 1.30Z_t + .00(\theta_t - \phi_t)\overline{P}_t \quad \delta = .65, \text{Rep} = 8$$

These results suggest that processes that differ only in how they move from one equilibrium to the next or in the sequence of exogenous shocks may generate data that give quite different pictures of the underlying process. This outcome creates considerable uncertainty about the reliability of traditional methods for estimating path-dependent processes where only the equilibrium outcomes are observed.

E. Vector Autoregression Models

The final comparison is to apply VAR methods to simulated data sets generated with models with endogenous preferences. The three replications shown above have been selected for this analysis, as there is no concise way to conduct and summarise the results of a VAR estimation on all twenty replications. The structural estimations for $\overline{X}_t$ in these three replications imply contrary exogenous influences so it will be interesting to see what patterns are discovered by the VAR method. The contemporaneous values of each variable were regressed against Z_t and $\overline{X}_{t-1}$, and lagged values of itself and the other variables. A series of F-tests were conducted on sets of these variables to determine if there were any possibly significant relationships.

REFERENCES

Achen, C.H. 1983. Toward theories of data: the state of political methodology. Pp. 69-94 in *Political Science: The State of the Discipline,* ed. A. Finifter. Washington, D.C.: American Political Science Association.

Arthur, W. B.; Ermoliev, Y. M.; and Kaniovski, Y. M. 1987. Path-dependent processes and the emergence of macro-structure. *European Journal of Operational Research,* 30: 294-303.

Bartels L. M., and Brady, H. E. 1993. The state of quantitative political methodology. Pp. 121-58 in *Political Science: The State of the Discipline II,* ed. A. Finifter. Washington, D.C.: American Political Science Association.

Beck, N. 1983. Time-varying parameter regression models. *American Journal of Political Science, 27*:557-600.

Brady, H.M. 1993. Stability, reliability, and guessing. Paper presented at the Annual Meeting of the Midwest Political Science Association, Chicago, April 1993.

Carmines, E. C., and Stimson, J. A. 1989. *Issue Evolution: Race and the Transformation of American Politics.* Princeton, N.J.: Princeton University Press.

Dawson, M. 1992. *Behind the Mule.* Princeton, N.J.: Princeton University Press.

Erikson, R. S. 1979. The SRC panel data and mass political attitudes:

change and uncertainty. BririsA *Journal of Political Science,* 9:89-114.

Franklin, C. H. 1990. Estimation across datasets: two-stage auxiliary instrumental variables estimation (2SAIV). *Political Analysis,* 1:1-24.

Freeman, J. R. 1989. Systematic sampling, temporal aggregation, and the study of political relationships. *Political Analysis,* 1:61-98.

Gerber, E. R., and Jackson, J. E. 1993. Endogenous preferences and the study of institutions. *American Political Science Review,* 87:639-56

Hanushek, E. A., and Jackson, J. E. 1977. *Statistical Methods for Social Scientists.* New York: Academic Press.

Hibbs, D. A., Jr. 1974. Problems of statistical estimation and causal inference in time-series regression models. *Sociological Methodology,* 1973-74:252-308.

Jackson, J. E. 1973. *Constituencies and Leaders in Congress.* Cambridge, Mass.: Harvard University Press.

Joreskog, K. G. 1973. A general method for estimating a linear structural equation system. Pp. 85-112 in *Structural Equation Models in the Social Sciences,* ed. A. S. Goldberger and O. D. Duncan. New York: Seminar Press.

Judge, G. G.; Griffiths, W. E. ; Hill, R. C.; Lotkepohl, H.; and Lee, T. C. 1985. *The Theory and Practice of Econometrics.* 2nd edn. New York: Wiley.

Kellstedt, P.; McAvoY, G. E.; and Stimson, J. A. 1995. Dynamic analysis with latent constructs. *Political Analysis,* 5:113-50.

King, G. 1989a. *Unifying Political Methodology.* New York; Cambridge University Press.

Krugman, P. 1991. *Geography and Trade.* Cambridge, Mass.: MIT Press.

Markus, G. B. 1988. The impact of personal and national economic conditions on the presidential vote: a pooled cross-sectional analysis. *American Journal of Political Science,* 32:137-54.

McGinnis, M. D., and Williams, J. T. 1989. Change and stability in superpower rivalry. *American Political Science Review,* 83:1101-23.

North D. C. 1990. *Institutions, Institutional Change and Economic Performance.* Cambridge: Cambridge University Press.

Page, B. I., and Jones, C. C. 1979. Reciprocal effects of policy preferences, party loyalties and the vote. *American Political Science Review,* 73:1071-89.

Riker, W. H., and Weimer, D. L. 1993. The economic and political liberalisation of socialism: the fundamental problem of property rights. *Social Philosophy and Policy,* 10: 79-102.

Rivers, D. 1988. Heterogeneity in models of electoral choice. *American Journal of Political Science,* 32:737-57.

Smith, R. M., and Box-Steffensmier, J.M, 1995. The macrofoundations of aggregate partisanship: a fractional integration analysis of heterogeneity and permanence. *American Political Science Review,* forthcoming.

Williams, J.T., and McGinnis, M. D. 1988. Sophisticated reaction in the U.S.-Soviet arms race: evidence of rational expectations. *American Journal of Political Science,* 32:968-95.

9

Miscellaneous Theories

> "A zealous soul without meekness is like a ship in a storm, in danger of a wrecks. A meek soul without zeal is like a ship in a calm, that moves not so fast as it ought."
>
> —***James M. Mason***

After having an elaborate discussion of all important political theories in preceding chapters, now we will highlight some more political theories. Definitely this will enlighten the users of the book.

First we come to dual presidency theory.

I. DUAL PRESIDENCY THEORY

The Dual Presidency Theory (also sometimes referred to as the 'Two Presidencies Thesis') is a theory proposed by the political scientist Aaron Wildavsky during the Cold War. Influenced by the time period of 1946-1964, the Dual Presidency Theory is based on the principle that there are two versions of the American President: one who is concerned with domestic policy and one concerned with foreign policy. Wildavsky makes the claim that Presidents would prefer to focus foremost on foreign policy because he is granted more traditional, constitutional, and statutory authority when compared to his domestic policy powers. Wildavsky argues that presidents have assumed a more active role with regards to foreign policy because they are able to act more quickly than the United States Congress when pursuing foreign policy.

Also, a lack of interest groups active in foreign policy allow the president more discretion when making a decision. However, since Wildavsky's time, the domestic impact of foreign policy has become more pronounced and important, blurring the lines between foreign and domestic affairs. Politics no longer stop at the waters edge because Congress receives more reliable information on foreign affairs. Foreign policy is very much controlled by partisan politics in the United States today. Presidents no longer may take the liberty to assume public support for his foreign policy initiatives and must strive to build and maintain domestic support for them instead.

II. PUBLIC ADMINISTRATION THEORY

Public administration theory is the amalgamation of history, organizational theory, social theory, political theory and related studies focused on the meanings, structures and functions of public service in all its forms.

A standard course of study in PhD programs dedicated to public administration, public administration theory often recounts major historical foundations for the study of bureaucracy as well as epistemological issues associated with public service as a profession and as an academic field.

Important figures of study often include the following persons: Max Weber, Frederick Taylor, Luther Gulick, Mary Parker Follett, Chester Barnard, Herbert Simon, and Dwight Waldo. In more recent times, the field has had three main branches: new public management, classic public administration and postmodern public administration theory. The last grouping is often viewed as manifest in the Public Administration Theory Network (PAT-NET) and its publication, *Administrative Theory & Praxis*.

Important Works in the History of Public Administration Theory

- The Northcote-Trevelyan Report
- Pendleton Act of 1883
- The Study of Administration, Woodrow Wilson, 1887
- Politics as a Vocation, 1918, Bureaucracy, 1922, Max Weber
- Functions of the Executive, Chester Barnard
- The Brownloe Commission Report
- The Lack of a Budgetary Theory, V.O. Key, Jr., 1940
- Bureaucracy, Ludwig von Mises, 1944
- The Administrative State, Dwight Waldo, 1948
- Administrative Behavior, Herbert A. Simon, 1953
- TVA and the Grass Roots, Philip Selznick, 1953
- The Science of Muddling Through, Charles E. Lindblom, 1959
- The Forest Ranger, Herbert Kaufman, 1960.
- Democracy and the Public Service, Frederick C. Mosher, 1968
- Servant Leadership, Robert K. Greenleaf
- Organisation theory : Revisiting The Elephant", Public Administration Review , Dwight Waldo,1978
- Public and Private Management: Are They Alike in All the Unimportant Respects?, Graham T. Allison, 1980
- The New Economics of Organization, American Journal of Political Science, Terry M. Moe, 1984
- Organizational Design as Policy Analysis, Policy Studies Journal, Karen M. Hult and Charles Walcott 1989
- Refounding Public Administration, Gary Wamsley ed., 1990
- Street Level Bureaucracy, Michael Lipsky
- The Public Administration Theory Primer, H. George Frederickson and Kevin B. Smith, 2003
- The Case for Bureaucracy, Charles Goodsell

III. SAFETY VALVE THEORY

The safety valve theory was a theory about how to deal with unemployment which gave rise to the Homestead Act of 1862 in the United States. Given the concentration of immigrants (and population) on the Eastern coast, it was hypothesized that making free land available in the West, would relieve the pressure for employment in the East. By analogy with steam pressure (= the need for work), the enactment of a free land law, it was believed, would act as a safety valve. A distinction has to be made between (1) the safety valve theory as an ideal and (2) the safety valve theory as embodied in the Homestead Act of 1862.

There is a dispute whether and to what extent the Homestead Act did or did not succeed as a safety valve in ameliorating the problem of unemployment in the East. Opposition to giving away free land came from employers, who anticipated either a shortage of employees or conditions favorable to employees.

IV. SELECTORATE THEORY

The selectorate theory is detailed in *The Logic of Political Survival*, authored by Bruce Bueno de Mesquita of New York University (NYU), Alastair Smith of NYU, Randolph M. Siverson of UC Davis, James D. Morrow of the University of Michigan. The theory operates on two fundamental groups, the Winning Coalition and the Selectorate, both drawn from the overall populace of a state.

The Winning Coalition is a subset of the Selectorate, and the Selectorate is a subset of the overall population. The Selectorate is simply those within the state that have a say in policy outcome, in the United States, for example, it would be all citizens over the age of 18 eligible to vote.

The Winning Coalition is a portion of the Selectorate sufficient to choose and sustain a leader in office.

Distribution of Goods

A public good is such a good that everyone non-exclusively enjoys, such as national defense. The public good in this example would be the security provided to citizens of a state. A private good is a good that is enjoyed exclusively by a select few, usually within the Winning Coalition, and cannot be shared. An example of such a good would be anything exclusionary, such as food surpluses.

It can be said, then, that everyone in the Selectorate, including the Winning Coalition, reap the benefits of public goods while only those within the Winning Coalition enjoy private goods.

Government Types, Leaders, and Challenger Threats

According to the selectorate theory, a leader has the greatest chance of political survival when the Selectorate is large and the Winning Coalition is small, an autocracy. This is because those who are in a winning coalition can easily be replaced by other members of the selectorate who are not in the Winning Coalition. Thus, the costs of defection for those members of the Winning Coalition can be potentially large, namely the loss of all private goods. Similarly, the chances of a challenger in replacing the leader are similarly smallest in such an autocratic system since those in the winning coalition would be hard pressed to defect.

Private goods are highest in such a system vis-à-vis public goods. In a monarchy, where the Selectorate is small and the Winning Coalition is even smaller, provides the challenger with a greater opportunity to overthrow the current leader. This is because the proportion of Selectorate members who are also in the Winning Coalition is relatively large. That is to say if a new leader comes to power, chances are a given member of the Winning Coalition will remain within the coalition.

The incentive for defection in order to attain a greater amount of goods offered by a challenger is not, in this case, outweighed by the risk of not being included in the new Winning Coalition. Here, the proportion of private goods in relation to public goods is seen declining. A scenario where both the Winning Coalition is large and the Selectorate is even larger provides the least amount of stability to a leader's occupancy of power, such a system is a Democracy. Here, the proportion of public goods outweigh private goods simply because of the sheer size of the Winning Coalition; it would be far too costly to provide private goods to every individual member of the Winning Coalition when the benefits of public goods would be enjoyed by all. Because of this fact — that the leader cannot convince Winning Coalition members to remain loyal through private good incentives, which are in turn cost-restrictive, the challenger poses the greatest threat to the incumbent. Furthermore, this degree of loyalty to the incumbent leader, whatever the government structure may be, is called the Loyalty Norm.

Remarkably, a scenario where the Winning Coalition is large and the Selectorate is small is logically impossible since the Winning Coalition is a subset of the Selectorate.

V. SINGLE-MINDEDNESS THEORY

The single-mindedness theory (SMT) studies the effects of social groups' preferences on the political equilibria and affirms that those groups which are more able to focus on the minimum number of issues gain a greater political power which enables them to eventually get what they require.

The theory represents one of the most remarkable examples of political failure in the attempt to achieve the welfare of society. In full accordance with Buchanan's vision of governments as "Leviathans" and using political competition models which exploit the probabilistic voting model approach, the theory demonstrates how those groups which dissipate their mindedness over a great number of issues are more vulnerable to the political action of more focalized and single-minded groups.

The main feature characterizing a SMT model is the existence of an endogenous density function in the political candidate maximand which shape the distribution of the so-called "swing voters" (those voters who do not have any particular preference for any candidate) and determines the magnitude of these voters' migration toward one or another candidate as a result of a change in the government's policy. Individuals have political preferences, whose degree of homogeneity is captured by a density function which is monotonically increasing in the consumption of goods (or leisure as in Sala-i-Martin and Mulligan's model). The density function represents a proxy for the political power of a group, since more ideologically homogeneous groups are more politically successful.

Pioneer economists who started to deal with the single-mindedness issues were Mulligan and Sala-i-Martin (1999) and Profeta (2002).

One of the pros of the SMT is represented by its broad applicability in many fields of social economics: labor market, pension systems, environmental policies, distribution of lands, secessions, division of powers, industrial policies and many others. Another advantage of the theory is its ability to suggest possible solution to political failures: reducing the power of single-minded groups by increasing the mindedness of more disadvantaged groups (i.e. via the constitution of associative organizations) would help them to increase the political power of these groups and thus to enable governments to undertake more redistributive policies. The theory was also used to find several formulae which aim to describe the way politicians tax in the real world.

VI. STATE CENTERED THEORY

State centred theory is a political theory which stresses the role of the government on civil society. It holds that the state itself can structure political life to some degree independently of the way power is distributed between classes and other groups at a given time.

VII. POLITICAL THEOLOGY

Political theology or public theology is a branch of both political philosophy and theology that investigates the ways in which theological concepts or ways of thinking underlie political, social, economic and cultural discourses.

The same term has been used in a wide variety of ways by writers exploring different aspects of the subject, with tension developing between those advocating a traditional concern with individual "moral reform", such as Clyde Wilcox's *God's Warriors* (1992) and Ted Jelen's *The Political World of the Clergy* (1993), and those on the left who focus on collective "social justice" e.g. Jeffrey K. Hadden's *The Gathering Storm in the Churches* (1969) and Harold Quinley's *The Prophetic Clergy* (1974).

Writing amidst the turbulence of the German Weimar

Republic Carl Schmitt, in *Political Theology*, argued that the central concepts of modern politics were secularized versions of older theological concepts. Drawing on Thomas Hobbes in *Leviathan* he argued that the state exists to maintain its own integrity in order to ensure order in society in times of crisis.

The journal *Political Theology* currently examines this interface of religious faith and politics.

The Catholic theologian Johann Baptist Metz explored the concept of *political theology* throughout his work. He argued for the concept of a 'suffering God' who shared the pain of his creation, writing, "Yet, faced with conditions in God's creation that cry out to heaven, how can the theology of the creator God avoid the suspicion of apathy unless it takes up the language of a suffering God?"

VIII. PRIVATE-COLLECTIVE MODEL OF INNOVATION

The term private-collective model of innovation was coined by Eric von Hippel and Georg von Krogh in their 2003 publication in Organization Science. This innovation model represents a combination of the private investment model and the collective-action innovation model.

In the private investment model innovators appropriate financial returns from innovations through intellectual property rights such as patents, copyright, licenses, or trade secrets. Any knowledge spillover reduces the innovator's benefits, thus freely revealed knowledge is not in the interest of the innovator. The collective-action innovation model explains the creation of public goods which are defined by the non-rivalry of benefits and non-excludable access to the good. In this case the innovators do not benefit more than any one else not investing into the public good, thus free-riding occurs. In response to this problem, the cost of innovation has to be distributed, therefore governments typically invest into public goods through public funding. As combination of the these two models the private-collective model of innovation explains the creation of public goods through private funding.

The model is based on the assumption that the innovators privately creating the public goods benefit more than the free-riders only consuming the public good. While the result of the investment is equally available to all, the innovators benefit through the *process* of creating the public good. Therefore, private-collective innovation occurs when the process-related rewards exceed the process-related costs.

The development of open source software / Free Software (consequently named Free and Libre Open Source Software - FLOSS) is the most prominent example of private-collective innovation. By definition, FLOSS represents a public good. It is non-rival because copying and distributing software does not decrease its value. And it is non-excludable because FLOSS licenses enable everyone to use, change and redistribute the software without any restriction. While FLOSS is created by many unpaid individuals it has been shown that technology firms invest substantially in the development of FLOSS. These companies release previously proprietary software under FLOSS licenses, employ programmers to work on established FLOSS projects, and fund entrepreneurial firms to develop certain features. In this way, private entities invest into the creation of public goods.

IX. POWER VACUUM

Basically power vacuum is an expression for a political situation that can occur when a government has no identifiable central authority. The metaphor implies that, like a physical vacuum, other forces will tend to "rush in" to fill the vacuum as soon as it is created, perhaps in the form of an armed militia or insurgents, military coup, warlord or dictator.

Historian Fernand Braudel compared the situation of Italy during the Renaissance as a "cyclonic zone, an enormous vacuum", which would sweep in foreign armies:

> "The strength of the barriers in eastern and south-western Europe varied from century to century. The nomads' worlds rotated between these areas of negligence, weakness and sometimes ineffectual vigilance. A physical law drew them now westwards, now eastwards, according to whether their explosive life would ignite more easily in Europe, Islam, India or China. Eduard Fueter's classic work drew attention to a cyclonic zone, an enormous vacuum in 1494 over the fragmented Italy of princes and urban republics. All Europe was attracted towards this storm-creating area of low pressure. In the same way hurricanes persistently blew the people of the steppes eastwards or westwards according to the lines of least resistance.

During or following a civil war there is often a power vacuum of some sort. For example, the war-torn nation of Somalia is currently mired in a power vacuum, with no central government or president exercising control over the supposed "Republic of Somalia".

A power vacuum can also occur following a constitutional crisis in which large portions of the government resign or are removed, creating unclear issues regarding succession to positions of power.

After the World War II, there was a power vacuum in Europe. Along with the division of East and West Germany, Stalin's diplomacy and governance, the development of the atomic bomb, policies of containment of communism, the expansionism of the USSR and a growing lack of trust (fear of a hegemony) were seen to be factors in the emergence of the Cold War. More recently, the tight control which Saddam Hussein's Baath party exerted on Iraq could have been exploited during a transitional hand-over period following the 2003 invasion of Iraq. Instead, the US Government's policy of purging Baath party members from the Iraqi government after the invasion created a power vacuum which was quickly filled by insurgents, who then began to attack American service personnel using improvised explosive devices and snipers.

The general concept of a "power vacuum" is relevant to many personal and organizational situations. In the criminal world many drug lords are able to become untouchable because of fear of any backlash occurring in a power vacuum situation.

X. POST-DEMOCRACY

It is significant to note that term Post-democracy designates a State conducted by democratic rules, but whose application is progressively limited. The English conservative journalist Peter Oborne presented a documentary of the 2005 general election, arguing that it had become anti-democratic because it targeted a number of floating voters with a narrow agenda.

This term appeared to define a running evolution within the democracies during the 21st century.

It is a polemic term because it calls attention to recognised democracies that are losing some of their foundations evolving toward an Aristocratic regime.

A *Post-democracy* may be characterised with:

(a) non representative elections

(b) citizen rights are not respected by the state, or its representatives

(c) or, impossibility to get balanced debates

Hereby, while thus contradicting pluralist assumptions, it seems to be an accepted presumption, that the common good were something to be determined objectively and that conflicts of interest were not to be handled within democratic processes but instead within administrative proceedings.

XI. POWER RESOURCE THEORY

Power resource theory is a political theory which proposes the idea that the distribution of power between major classes is to some extent accountable for the successes and failure of various political ideologies. It argues that "at its core, it asserts that working class power achieved through organisation by labor unions or left parties, produces more egalitarian distributional outcomes"

REFERENCES

Democratizing innovation (2005) Eric von Hippel, MIT Press

Eric von Hippel and Georg von Krogh (2003) "Open Source Software and the 'Private-Collective' Innovation Model: Issues for Organization Science" *Organization Science* 14, 209-223.

Eric von Hippel and Georg von Krogh "Free revealing and the private-collective model of innovation incentives", *R&D Management,* 36(3), 2006, pp. 295-306.

Fernand Braudel, *Capitalism and Material Life*, New York, Harper & Row, 1967, vol. I, p.57

Georg von Krogh (2008) "Researching the Private-Collective Innovation Model" *The SAGE Handbook of New Approaches in Management and Organization,* Daved Barry and Hans Hansen (ed.) Sage, pp. 396-397.

"Johann-Baptist Metz", *The Vocabulary of Political Theology*, Gonzaga University.

Matthias Stuermer, Sebastian Spaeth, and Georg von Krogh, G. (2009) "Extending private-collective innovation: a case study" *R&D Management* 39(2), 170-191.

"Political Theology: Four Chapters on the Concept of Sovereignty", Carl Schmitt, University of Chicago Press.

"Political Theology", Open Source Journals, Equinox Publishing.

Williams, Rhys H. "Political Theology on the Right and Left", *Religion Online*.

Appendix

LEADING OF POLITICAL SCIENCE JOURNALS

- The Acorn: Journal of the Gandhi-King Society
- *American Journal of Political Science*
- *American Political Science Review*
- *American Politics Research*
- *Annual Review of Political Science*
- *Australian Quarterly*
- *British Journal of Political Science*
- *British Journal of Politics and International Relations*
- *Canadian Journal of Political Science*
- *Comparative Political Studies*
- *Comparative Politics*
- *European Political Economy Review*
- *Evidence & Policy*
- *Foreign Policy*
- *Foreign Affairs*
- *Government and Opposition*
- *International Affairs*
- *International Affairs Review*
- *Journal for Peace and Justice Studies*

- *Journal of Common Market Studies*
- *Journal of Conflict Resolution*
- *Journal of Contingencies and Crisis Management*
- *Journal of Democracy*
- *Journal of International Policy Solutions*
- *Journal of Information Technology & Politics*
- *Journal of Moral Philosophy*
- *Journal of Peace Research*
- *Journal of Politics*
- *Journal of Politics & Society*
- *Economic and Political Weekly*
- *Michigan Journal of Political Science*
- *Peace Review*
- *Policy & Politics*
- *Policy Sciences*
- *Perspectives on Politics*
- *Politica*
- *Political Analysis*
- *Political Behavior*
- *Political Geography*
- *The Political Quarterly*
- *Political Psychology*
- *Political Science Forum*
- *Political Science Quarterly*
- *Political Studies*
- *Political Studies Review*

- *Politics and Policy*
- *Politics & Society*
- *Politikon: The IAPSS Journal of Political Science*
- *PS Political Science & Politics*
- *Public Administration and Development*
- *Publius*
- *Radical Philosophy Review*
- *Research on Democracy and Society*
- *Review of Politic*
- *Revista de Ciencia Política*
- *Social Philosophy Today*
- *Social Theory and Practice*
- *World Political Science Review*
- *Yale Journal of International Affairs*

Bibliography

Allen, A. 1988. *Uneasy Access: Privacy far Women in a Free Society*. Totowa, N.J.: Rowman and Littlefield.

Arato, A., and Cohen, J. 1992. *Civil Society and Political Theory*. Cambridge, Mass.: MIT Press.

Arendt, H. 1958. *The Human Condition*. Chicago: University of Chicago Press.

Arthur, J., and Shaw, W., eds. 1978. *Justice and Economic Distribution*. Englewood Cliffs, N.J.: Prentice-Hall.

Arthur, W. B.; Ermoliev, Y. M.; and Kaniovski, Y. M. 1987. Path-dependent processes and the emergence of macro-structure. *European Journal of Operational Research,* 30: 294-303.

Bacchi, C. 1991. *Same Difference*. Boston: Alien and Unwin.

Barber, B. 1984. *Strong Democracy*. Berkeley; University of California Press.

Barry, B. 1979. The strange death of political philosophy. Pp. 11-23 in *Democracy, Power and Justice*. Oxford: Clarendon Press, 1989.

Bay, C. 1981. *Strategies of Political Emancipation*. Notre Dame, Ind.: University of Notre Dame Press.

Beck, N. 1983. Time-varying parameter regression models. *American Journal of Political Science, 27*:557-600.

Beitz, C. 1979. *Political Theory and International Relations*.

Princeton: Princeton University Press.

Bernstein, R. 1986. Rethinking the social and the political. Pp. 238-59 in R. Bernstein, *Philosophical Profiles.* Philadelphia, Pp.: University of Pennsylvania Press.

Bobbio, N. 1984. *The Future of Democracy.* Minneapolis: University of Minnesota Press.

Bock, G., and James, S., eds. 1992. *Beyond Equality and Difference.* London: Routledge.

Boggs, C. 1986. *Social Movements and Political Power.* Philadelphia, Pa.: Temple University Press.

Bohman, J. 1996. *Public Deliberation.* Cambridge, Mass.: MIT Press.

Bowis, N., 1988, *Equal Opportunity.* Boulder, Colo.: Westview Press.

Boxill, B. 1984 *Blacks and Social Justice.* Totowa, N.J.: Rowman and Allenheld.

Brown, W. 1988. *Manhood and Politics.* Totowa, N.J.: Rowman and Littlefield.

Burchell, G.; Gordon, C.; and Miller, P., eds. 1991. *The Foucault Effect.* Chicago: University of Chicago Press.

Burnheim, J. 1985, *Is Democracy Possible?* Oxford: Polity Press.

Calhoun, C. ed 1991. *Habermas and the Public Sphere.* Cambridge, Mass.: MIT Press.

Canovan, M. 1992. *Hannah Arendt: A Reinterpretation of Her Political Thought.* Cambridge: Cambridge University Press.

Caraway, N. 1991. *Segregated Sisterhood.* Nashville: University of Tennesee Press.

Carens, J.H. 1993. Citizenship and aboriginal self-government. Ottawa, Ont.: Royal Commission on Aboriginal Peoples.

Clark, L., and Lange, L. 1979. *The Sexism of Social and Political Theory.* Toronto: University of Toronto Press.

Cohen, J. 1983. Class and Civil Society. Amherst: University of Massachusetts Press.

Connolly, W.E. 1987. *Politics and Ambiguity.* Madison: University of Wisconsin Press.

Cunningham, F. 1987. *Democratic Theory and Socialism.* Cambridge: Cambridge University Press.

Dallmayr, F. 1981. *Twilight of Subjectivity.* Amherst: University of Massachusetts Press.

Dani, R.A. 1985. *A Preface to Economic Democracy.* Berkeley: University of California Press.

Dawson, M. 1992. *Behind the Mule.* Princeton, N.J.: Princeton University Press.

Dayzek, J. 1987. *Rational Ecology.* Oxford: Basil Blackwell.

Democratizing innovation (2005) Eric von Hippel, MIT Press

Elshtain, J.B. 1981. *Public Man, Private Woman.* Princeton, N.J.: Princeton University Press.

Erikson, R. S. 1979. The SRC panel data and mass political attitudes: change and uncer-tainty. BririsA *Journal of Political Science,* 9:89-114.

Ezorsky, G. 1991. *Racism and Justice,* Ithaca, N.Y.: Cornell University Press.

Fernand Braudel, *Capitalism and Material Life*, New York, Harper & Row, 1967, vol. I, p.57

Fishkin, J.S. 1991. *Deliberative Democracy.* New Haven, Conn.: Yale University Press, 1991.

Fisk, M. 1989. *The State and Justice.* Cambridge: Cambridge University Press.

Foucault, M. 1979. *Discipline and Punish,* trans. A Sheridan. New York: Vintage Books.

Fraser, N. 1989. *Unruly Practices.* Minneapolis: University of Minnesota Press.

Freeman, J. R. 1989. Systematic sampling, temporal aggregation, and the study of political relationships. *Political Analysis,* 1:61-98.

Galston, W. 1991. *Liberal Purposes.* Cambridge: Cambridge University Press.

Goldman, A. 1979. *Justice and Reverse Discrimination.* Princeton, N.J.: Princeton University Press.

Goodin, R.E. 1988. *Reasons for Welfare.* Princeton, N.J.: Princeton University Press.

Goodin, R.E. 1992. *Green Political Theory.* Oxford: Polity Press.

Green, P. 1985. *Retrieving Democracy.* Totowa, N.J.: Rowman and Allenheld.

Gutmamn. A. 1980. *Liberal Equality.* Cambridge: Cambridge University Press.

Hanushek, E. A., and Jackson, J. E. 1977. *Statistical Methods for Social Scientists.* New York: Academic Press.

Hartsock, N. 1983. *Money. Sex and Power.* New York: Longman.

Held, V. 1987. Non-contractual society. Pp. 111-38 in *Science, Morality and Feminist Theory,* ed. M. Hanen and K. Nielsen. Calgary: University of Calgary Press.

Hirst, P. 1990. *Representative Democracy and its Limits.* Oxford: Polity Press.

Honig, B. 1993. *Political Theory and the Displacement of Politics.* Ithaca, N.Y.: Cornell University Press.

Honneth, A. 1991. *The Critique of Power.* Cambridge, Mass.: MIT Press.

Jackson, J. E. 1973. *Constituencies and Leaders in Congress.* Cambridge, Mass.: Harvard University Press.

Jones, K. 1993. *Compassionate Authority.* New York Routledge.

Judge, G. G.; Griffiths, W. E. ; Hill, R. C.; Lotkepohl, H.; and Lee, T. C. 1985. *The Theory and Practice of Econometrics.* 2nd edn. New York: Wiley.

Keane, J. 1984. *Public Life in Late Capitalism.* Cambridge: Cambridge University Press.

Kellstedt, P.; McAvoY, G. E.; and Stimson, J. A. 1995. Dynamic analysis with latent con-structs. *Political Analysis,* 5:113-50.

King, G. 1989a. *Unifying Political Methodology.* New York; Cambridge University Press.

Kipnis, K., and Meyers, D. T., eds. 1985. *Economic Justice: Private Rights and Public Responsibilities.* Totowa, N.J.: Rowman and Allenheld.

Krugman, P. 1991. *Geography and Trade.* Cambridge, Mass.: MIT Press.

Kymlicka, W. 1989. *Liberalism, Community and Culture.* Oxford: Clarendon Press.

Laclau, E., and Mouffe, C. 1985. *Hegemony and Socialist Strategy.* London: Verso.

Landes, J. 1988. *Women and the Public Sphere in the Age*

of the French Revolution. Ithaca, N.Y.: Cornell University Press.

Lawson, B., and McGary, H. 1992. *Between Slavery and Freedom.* Bloomington: Indiana University Press.

Lefort, C. 1986. *The Political Forms of Modem Society.* Cambridge: Cambridge University Press.

Lyotard, I.-F. 1984. *The Postmodern Condition.* Minneapolis: University of Minnesota Press.

Macedo, S. 1990. *Liberal Virtues.* Cambridge, Mass.: Harvard University Press.

MacIntyre, A. 1981. *After Virtue.* Notre Dame, Ind.: Notre Dame University Press.

Mackuen, m.b.; erikson, R. S.; and Stimson, J. A. 1989. Macropartisanship. *American Political Science Review,* 83:1125-42.

Macpherson, C. B. 1973. *Democratic Theory.* Oxford: Clarendon Press.

Mansbridge, I. J. 1980. *Beyond Adversary Democracy.* New York Basic Books.

Melucci, A. 1989. *Nomads of the Present* London: Hutchinson Radius.

Michelman, F. 1986. Traces of self-government. *Harvard Law Review,* 100:1-311.

Miller, D. 1976. *Social Justice.* Oxford: Clarendon Press.

Miller, J. 1984. *Rousseau: Dreamer of Democracy.* New Haven, Conn.: Yale University Press.

Mouffe, C. 1993. *The Return of the Political.* London: Verso.

Nicholson, L. 1986. *Gender and History.* New York: Columbia University Press.

Nielsen, K. 1985. *Equality and Liberty.* Totowa, N.J.: Rowaman and Allanheld.

North D. C. 1990. *Institutions, Institutional Change and Economic Performance.* Cambridge: Cambridge University Press.

Nozick, R. 1974. *Anarchy, State and Utopia.* New York: Basic Books.

O'Neili, O. 1986. *Faces of Hunger.* London: Allen and Unwin.

Offe, C. 1984. *Contradictions of the Welfare State.* Cambridge, Mass.: MIT Press.

Okin, S.M. 1988. *The Sexual Contract.* Standord, Calif.: Stanford University Press.

Phillips, A. 1991. *Engendering Democracy.* University Park, Penn : Penn State Press.

Pitkin, H.F. 1984. *Fortune is a Woman.* Berkeley: University of California Press.

Rawls, J. 1971. *A Theory of Justice.* Cambridge, Mass.: Harvard University Press.

Reiman, J. 1990. *Justice and Modern Moral Theory.* New Haven, Conn.: Yale University Press.

Riker, W. H., and Weimer, D. L. 1993. The economic and political liberalisation of social-ism: the fundamental problem of property rights. *Social Philosophy and Policy,* 10: 79-102.

Rivers, D. 1988. Heterogeneity in models of electoral choice. *American Journal of Political Science,* 32:737-57.

Sagoff, M. 1988. *The Economy of the Earth.* Cambridge: Cambridge University Press.

Sandel, M.J. 1982. *Liberalism and the Limits of Justice.* Cambridge : Cambridge University Press.

Schweickart, D. 1980. *Capitalism or Worker Control?* New York: Paeger.

Scorrr, J.W. 1988. Deconstructing equality versu difference: or, the uses of poststructuralist theory for feminism. *Feminist Studies,* 14: 33-50.

Sen, A.K. 1992. *Inequality Reconsidered.* Oxford: Oxford University Press.

Shanley, M.L., and Pateman, C., eds. 1991. *Feminist Interpretations and Political Theory.* University Park, Pa.: Penn State Press.

Sharp, A. 1990. *Justice and the Maori.* Auckland: Oxford University Press.

Shklar, J. 1991. *American Citizenship.* Cambridge, Mass.: Harvard University Press.

Shue, H. 1980. *Basic Rights.* Princeton, N.J.: Princeton University Press.

Smart, B. 1983. *Foucault, Marxism and Critique.* London: Routledge and Kegan Paul.

Smith, R. M., and Box-Steffensmier, J.M. 1995. The macrofoundations of aggregate partisanship: a fractional integration analysis of heterogeneity and permanence. *American Political Science Review,* forthcoming.

Smith, R. 1989. "One united people:" second-class female citizenship and the American quest for community. *Yale Journal of Law and Humanities,* 1/2:229-93.

Spelman, E. 1988. *Inessential Woman.* Boston: Beacon Press.

Spivak, G.C. 1992. More on power/knowledge. Pp. 149-73

in *Rethinking Power,* ed. T.E. Wartenberg. Albany: State University of New York Press.

Spragens, T. 1990. *Reason and Democracy.* Durham, N.C.: Duke University Press.

Sterba, J. 1988. How to *Make People Just.* Totowa, N.J.: Rowman and Littlefield

Stiehm, J., ed. 1984. *Women's Views of the Political World of Men.* Dobbs Ferry, N.Y.: Transnational Publishers.

Sunstein, C. 1988. Beyond the republican revival. *Yale Law Journal,* 97:1539-90.

Taylor, C. 1984. Foucault on freedom and truth. *Political Theory,* 12:152-83.

Wallach, J. 1987. Liberalism, communitarians and the tasks of political theory. *Political Theory,* 15: 581-611.

Walzer, M. 1977. *Just and Unjust Wars.* New York: Basic Books.

Wartenberg, T. 1990. *Forms of Power.* Philadelphia, Pa.: Temple University Press.

Wellmam, C. 1982. *Welfare Rights.* Totowa, N.J.: Rowman-and Allenheld.

White, S. 1991. *Political Theory and Postmodernism.* Cambridge: Cambridge University Press.

Williams, J.T., and McGinnis, M. D. 1988. Sophisticated reaction in the U.S.-Soviet arms race: evidence of rational expectations. *American Journal of Political Science,* 32:968-95.

Wilson, M., and Yeatman, A., eds. 1995. *Justice and Identity.* Wellington, N.Z.: Bridget Williams.

Williams, R. A. 1990. *The American Indian in Western Legal Thought.* Oxford: Oxford

Yeatman, A. 1994. *Postmodern Revisionings of the Political.* New York: Routledge.

Young, I.M. 1987. *Impartiality and the civic public: some implications of feminist critiques of moral and political theory*. Pp. 56-76 in (ed.) S. Benhabib and D. Cornell. Minneapolis: University of Minnesota Press.

Index

●●●